AUSTIN AND ROVER METRO
THE FULL STORY

CRAIG CHEETHAM

AMBERLEY

First published 2020

Amberley Publishing
The Hill, Stroud,
Gloucestershire, GL5 4EP

www.amberley-books.com

Copyright © Craig Cheetham, 2020

The right of Craig Cheetham to be identified as the Author
of this work has been asserted in accordance with the
Copyrights, Designs and Patents Act 1988.

ISBN 978 1 3981 0093 0 (print)
ISBN 978 1 3981 0094 7 (ebook)

British Library Cataloguing in Publication Data.
A catalogue record for this book is available from the British Library.

Typeset in 10pt on 12pt Celeste.
Typesetting by Amberley Publishing
Printed in the UK.

Contents

Introduction

There are some cars that become part of the fabric of society. Models that aren't just cars but are part of the streetscape. Cars that everyone can relate to and of which they have abiding memories.

Metro – A British Car to Beat the World.

The Metro is one such vehicle. Over an eighteen-year lifecycle, where it was sold as an Austin, a Rover, an MG, a Vanden Plas, a brand-less Metro and even a Morris (as a van), the car evolved through five clear generations. In total, just over 2 million were sold, and for most of its life it was a permanent fixture in Britain's top ten sales charts.

It enjoyed success in Europe, too, with France and Italy being important export markets. After all, it was billed as the 'British Car to Beat the World', launched with a jingoistic marketing campaign where a fleet of Metros defended the White Cliffs of Dover from foreign infiltrators.

At last, Britain had a home-grown hatchback of which it could be proud. Why would you even consider a Fiat 127, VW Polo or a Renault 5 when there was a credible rival rolling off a production line in South-West Birmingham?

It's no overstatement to say that in 1980 the Metro saved Britain's car industry. It was the most important new British car since the Mini and it had to be a success – something it became despite a spectacular false start.

In this book we chart the history of the Metro, from its panic restyle shortly before its debut, to its ignominious demise following a disastrous Euro NCAP crash test as the Rover 100.

We also take a look at some of the more unusual Metros – production models, conversions and prototypes – along with a summary of its surprisingly illustrious career as both a track and rally car.

Today, the Metro is an up-and-coming classic, having evolved from being a disposable banger to becoming an inexpensive and characterful old-school icon that has won the hearts of enthusiasts that are often younger than the car itself. Metro is retro, and with that comes a sense of nostalgic coolness that has managed to transcend generations.

Yes, it was a car that had flaws, many and various. But it was also a car that touched many people's lives and continues to do so. If that's not a reason to celebrate its existence, then I don't know what is.

I really hope you enjoy this book as much as I enjoyed writing it, and as much as I've loved owning the six different Metros I've had over the years myself.

It would also be remiss of me not to thank Keith Adams and the fabulous web resource www.aronline.co.uk, which is an essential source of facts, history and fascinating anecdotes from the archives of the British car industry. There's no other resource quite like it for motoring historians and I'm extremely grateful to Keith for allowing me to use some of the site's content herein.

Craig Cheetham
Cambridgeshire
November 2019

CHAPTER 1

Metro – The Early Years

A small car slightly bigger than the Mini had been part of British Leyland's plan from the late 1960s, but it wasn't until 1974 that the idea began to really gain traction.

It was right in the heart of the fuel crisis, with the global car industry rapidly downsizing and creating models that were significantly more fuel efficient. It was also an extremely dark time for BL, which was mired in financial crisis and headed for what would have turned out to be bankruptcy were it not for government intervention.

In order to survive, the company's executives needed to prove to potential investors that they were ready to respond to what was a fast-growing part of the car industry – a decision that, for once, was BL making a sensible choice.

Its initial idea was to replace the Mini with a larger hatchback, codenamed ADO74. But that idea was shelved in 1973, with Leyland focusing all of its resources on the new Allegro saloon, a more avant-garde alternative to the dowdy Morris Marina.

But by late 1974, pressures were building both internally and externally to revisit the idea of a supermini, which led to ADO88, a slightly bigger car that would compete head-on with the Renault 5, a car that was rapidly gaining traction in Europe since its launch two years earlier.

Shortly before the project began, former Rover and Land Rover product guru Spen King had been appointed as BL's Head of Product Development, replacing former Triumph man Harry Webster. King appointed Charles Griffin to head the development of new Austin and Morris cars, which would cater for the 'everyman' market in which the company achieved most of its sales.

Advanced ADO88 styling study shows Metro lines starting to emerge.

King and Griffin were regularly challenged internally as to how they could make a supermini profitable, after all the Mini had proven how tough it was to make money out of small cars, no matter how popular they were.

But King was persuasive, and Griffin was an engineering genius, who had learned a lot from working alongside Mini creator Alec Issigonis (something that may explain the original Metro's bus-like driving position). Between them, the pair secured backing from BL's directors to pursue the idea of a Mini replacement – a slightly larger car that would be priced a little higher.

Indeed, size was everything as far as ADO88 was concerned. The Allegro, which was still relatively new at the time, was smaller than its main rivals, with the Ford Escort, Hillman Avenger and Vauxhall Viva all offering more metal for the money. As a result, the new car couldn't be too big as it might be perceived as an alternative, despite the Allegro's lack of a hatchback. Besides, the company was renowned for being a master of packaging thanks to Issigonis's saloon car designs in the 1960s, which had always offered more interior space than their rivals in a smaller footprint.

CAR magazine had quite a bit of inside info by the summer of 1979.

July 1979 *CAR* magazine captured Metro on test.

The front-wheel-drive ADO88 – so called because it was originally planned to have an 88-inch wheelbase, just like the Series II and III Land Rovers – would be packaged in such a way that it would equal its European rivals for flexibility.

The following year, though, disaster struck for British Leyland. Although outgoing boss John Barber had signed off on the 'New Mini', it was only after nationalisation and reassurance from the head of the UK's National Enterprise Board, Sir Don Ryder, that the government would foot the bill that work on the new project began in earnest. This time it was using public money – something that would ultimately stymie some of the more ambitious plans for the Metro, including a new overhead cam version of the A-Series engine known as the A-OHC.

With a need to prove development was moving fast, Charles Griffin told the board that ADO88 would be ready for market by the end of 1977, though it would be almost three years later when it finally reached fruition – something that was less Griffin's fault than that of internal deliberation. The original plan was to launch a car using as many carryover parts as possible from the Mini, but as more sophisticated superminis appeared on the market, including the new Ford Fiesta and VW Polo, it soon became apparent that the new car would need to be more advanced and unique in order to successfully compete.

Space efficiency was key to its design and also to it using BL's new 'Hydragas' suspension, which replaced Hydrolastic and had debuted on the Allegro, using nitrogen spheres to provide springing and thus reducing the space needed to install the car's subframes. Originally, the Hydragas system was supposed to be interlinked between front and rear, as on the Allegro, as this gave handling benefits as well as enhanced ride comfort. But much to the annoyance of the system's inventor, Dr Alex Moulton, the interlinked system was dropped before launch as a cost-cutting exercise.

Instead, the gas system was connected side to side to aid packaging and simplify the engineering required to install it, such was the eagerness to get the car to market.

More cost savings came with the powertrain. After the A-OHC project was shelved, a less involved reengineering of the A-Series engine took place to become the A-Plus unit, which was more powerful and efficient than the standard A-Series and would, critically, become available in sub 1.0-litre form in order to meet certain European tax requirements, something the Allegro's 1098cc unit couldn't offer.

Above left: Bonnet lines of ADO88 are clearly those of Metro. (AROnline)

Above right: Metro test mule undergoing winter testing.

The end of 1977 ticked by and there was still no production version of ADO88, though the front end was now clearly taking shape into what we now know as Metro. But there were further challenges ahead.

British Leyland was under new leadership, with South African businessman Michael Edwardes at the helm as the appointed Mr Fix-it and Harold Musgrove now in charge of product development. But with what was seemingly a sixth sense, Edwardes decided to bring in Rover chief stylist David Bache, fresh from the SD1 programme, to oversee the final touches.

A month later, in January 1978, Edwardes slammed the brakes on ADO88, despite what was seen to be an urgent need for the car by every stakeholder. In his 1983 memoir *Back from the Brink*, Edwardes recalled, 'There were very serious product defects and quality concerns. Yet this car was our lifeline. It needed to be properly executed.'

When Edwardes and the new Austin-Morris brand leader, Ray Horrocks, looked at the ADO88 for the first time in January 1978, both said it wasn't good enough, but it was too late for drastic changes. Their views were backed up by a dreadful showing in customer clinics, where ADO88 was seen as too basic, too cheaply finished and quite ugly compared to its sophisticated front-wheel-drive rivals as the supermini sector became the fastest growing area of the car market.

LC8 sketch shows how close the final Metro looked to styling team's vision.

LC8 vs rivals at a customer clinic. (AROnline)

The prototype's slab sides and near vertical tailgate may well have aided passenger space but did little for the Metro's appeal and meant an emergency restyle was ordered, with Bache in overall charge but with Allegro designer Harris Mann leading the design, backed by stylists Roger Tucker and Gordon Sked. The project was renamed LC8 to reflect the renaming of BL into Leyland Cars, and in little over a month the team had come up with a way of transforming the car's looks, but without too significant an effect on the engineering elements.

However, the cost of redesign was sufficient enough to cause other projects to fall by the wayside. The replacement Jaguar XJ was one, even though it (eventually the XJ40) was already substantially developed. The Jaguar would survive the cull, but only after the luxury brand became independent from Leyland in 1984. The two other projects that were waylaid – the Rover SD1 estate and the fully facelifted Allegro – never saw the light of day, though a mildly revised Allegro 3 did at least make Leyland's dumpling-shaped duckling slightly less ugly. Interestingly, until LC8 came along, the plan was for the new car to replace the Mini outright, but with the shift upmarket came a stay of execution for the company's smallest car which, ironically, was still in production when the Rover 100 was put out to pasture.

Late development prototype undergoes testing at MIRA test track in Leicestershire.

1979 and Metro is on test with disguised rear end.

Although it was Roger Tucker's restyled profile that was most visible in LC8, the Bache influences were also evident, including the SD1-style side swage lines and front valance, while the rear was given a more trapezoid angle, most likely as a result of Harris Mann's fondness of the shape.

Both Horrocks and Edwardes deemed the changes sufficient, and the LC8 was signed off, this time with a launch date planned for the British Motor Show in Birmingham in October 1980.

All that remained now was for the car to be given a name. Three were put forward – Maestro, Match and Metro – and were put to an employee ballot within Leyland Cars to determine a winner. Metro won, thanks in part to its urban nature, though by the time the car came out the name was changed to miniMetro as a result of a legal dispute with civil infrastructure company Metro Cammell.

At long last, Metro was good to go, and for the first time in years there was an air of genuine excitement around British motor manufacturing. The car was Leyland's Great White Hope; the future of the entire company resting on its slimline shoulders.

But could it really become the British car to beat the world?

Wind tunnel testing at MIRA in early 1980.

BL senior management undertake rival testing in 1979.

CHAPTER 2

1980 – A Bright New Dawn

'This is more than a car – it's a symbol to British industry.' With those words, Leyland's Product Chief, Harold Musgrove, pulled the wraps off BL's new baby, which made its media debut at the British Motor Show on October 11, 1980.

Musgrove, along with the rest of Leyland's senior management, was extremely upbeat about the new Metro, going on to describe it as 'the first of a new generation of cars that will, once again, make the British car industry one of the most competitive in Europe.'

It was a bold statement, but also a critical one as Leyland was already in the advanced stages of developing 'Project Bounty', the car that would become the Triumph Acclaim and the first in a crucial tie-in with Honda that would ultimately see the company being returned to private ownership. Being bold and confident was essential in order to keep investors happy as well as to drive forward the message that Leyland was taking quality seriously.

After all, its development had cost the British taxpayer £275 million, and the all-new body shop in which it was to be constructed was the most advanced automotive factory in the UK, with more robots and automated welders than any other car plant.

Above: The original Metro line-up, ready to take on the world.

Left: Launch brochure was plain and simple.

The launch was a strategically planned affair, with the UK's top motoring media being given advance access to Metros ahead of the big reveal under strict embargo. Public access to the new car came the following Monday, October 14, along with the first screening of the cliff-bound Metros chasing foreign imposters away, shown for the first time during the commercial break on the nation's most-watched soap opera, *Coronation Street*.

But how well received was the newcomer? The media were certainly upbeat, with *Motor* saying, 'Like the Mini before it, we can see it becoming a cult car. It looks chic, it is chic – but above all, it is *very* good.'

Autocar was similarly complimentary: 'To look at the Metro in-depth is to feel like Austin-Morris has done an outstandingly thorough job in all respects – design, development and production. Long-term experience will provide the final answers, but the auguries are good.'

But what was it that impressed the traditionally critical automotive media so much? Was it a sudden wave of patriotism, or something much more?

The answer is two-fold. First, the Metro was properly engineered, at least after the arrival of Michael Edwardes. The second was that, from mid-1979, the press had been given an unprecedented level of access to Leyland's senior managers and inner sanctum, allowing the company to tell its story in stages and involve the media in the car's development. Autocar even drove a pre-production model 5,000 miles across Europe, providing candid feedback to Leyland's engineers. It was a new approach and one that was a masterful piece of PR – not something for which the company was known in the past.

A launch-spec base model Metro in rather queasy Applejack Green.

Mud flaps were standard even on entry level car.

The media had spent much of the seventies 'BL-bashing', but there seemed to be a large amount of goodwill towards the Metro. After all, this was a car that had been paid for out of our taxes and there was a genuine hope that it would succeed.

It was of national importance for more than one reason as well – not only did it bring job security to Longbridge, but also to companies across the UK that were part of the supply chain. The sub frames, for example, came from Pressed Steel Fisher in Llanelli in a new £8 million factory, while body pressings came from the same company's Swindon plant. Brake linings came from Ferodo in Stockport, tyres were supplied by Goodyear in Wolverhampton and the new car was so critical to Lucas Automotive – with forty-one sites across the UK – that the company even wrote a song called *Hello Metro* to celebrate its launch. Oddly enough, it never made the charts.

The Metro, then, enjoyed one of the most rhapsodic launches of any British car ever made, but what did it mean on the showroom floor? Well, the dealers were certainly upbeat, though how much of this was down to Leyland's hospitality (see panel) and how much was down to the car itself was unclear.

But what they did have, for once, was a car they needn't make any apologies for. From the basic miniMetro to the range-topping HLS, the range had vast appeal.

The cabin was basic and functional at first.

Steering wheel was carried over from Allegro and Marina.

At its most basic, the £3,095 44 bhp miniMetro 1.0 had a minimalist honesty to it, with rubber bungs where plusher models had a rear wiper or cigarette lighter and blanking switches throughout the cabin. The cabin, meanwhile, was dominated by shiny embossed vinyl seats, though unlike some rivals the Metro was fully carpeted and came with a fold-down rear seat, along with a neat feature that allowed the parcel shelf to clip into the seat squab when in full load capacity mode. It also came with mud flaps as standard, where many rivals only offered them as an option even at the top of the range.

Next in line was the Metro L, which for an extra £400 gave the lucky buyer a heated rear screen, cloth trim, a trip meter, door pockets, armrests, grab handles, a rear wash-wipe and a 60:40 split-fold rear seat; quite a selling point in 1980. Plus, you could be sure your neighbours knew it wasn't a base Metro thanks to a twin coachline.

It was only a small jump of £200 extra, though, to be the proud custodian of a Metro HLE, which still used the 1.0-litre engine, but in 'high efficiency' form with an extra 2 bhp. It came with such luxuries as a cigar lighter, an analogue clock, a side rubbing strip and that status symbol of early eighties motoring, a push-button radio. It also gained one of the more distinguishable features of early Metros, with the lower models' inset headlamps being replaced by flush-fitting halogen lamp units with integral sidelights and indicators.

The top two models in the Metro range came with a 1.3-litre engine developing 63 bhp, which was quite peppy for its day, and came with two distinctive characters – sporting or luxury.

The 'sports' model, at least until 1982, was the Metro S, which had wide two-tone side stripes and unique 'herringbone' seat trim, along with seat valances to hide the lower frames. Tinted glass and a rev counter added to its racy appeal, along with a digital clock and a brake servo. The price of this desirable Metro for early adopters of the yuppie era? £3,995.

At the top of the tree, meanwhile, was the HLS, which was the only model to come as standard with a passenger door mirror, how times have changed! As well as the nearside mirror, it got brushed velour upholstery, head restraints, chrome wheel rim embellishers, velour door cards, a boot carpet, cloth-faced sun visors, a cloth headlining and a lockable fuel cap. But at £4,395, it was only £50 cheaper than an Allegro 1.7 HL or VW Golf 1.5 GLS, meaning it was really quite expensive for a supermini.

From a dealer's perspective, though, the entire Metro range was highly marketable, not least because of its class-leading luggage capacity of 45.68 cu. ft, thrifty fuel economy and previously unheard of 12,000-mile service intervals.

The seat belt and brake pad warning lights were only on early cars.

Four-speed gearbox was mounted in sump.

Original TV launch ad saw Metros chasing rivals away from White Cliffs of Dover.

Even with a few teething problems and some build quality issues on early cars – for which there really was no excuse – the all-new miniMetro was a fantastic seller, heading straight to the top three in the British sales charts, where it would remain for the duration of the first-generation Metro's life.

It continued to evolve, too, with a four-speed automatic joining the line-up in 1981 as a standalone model, and 1982 seeing the launch of a luxury Vanden Plas and a sporty version that saw the return of the illustrious MG marque, both of which have dedicated chapters elsewhere in this book. The miniMetro name was also dropped in December 1981, with Leyland having seemingly appeased Metro Cammell to use the name as a standalone.

In its best year on sale – 1983 – over 130,000 Metros were sold in the UK, almost two-thirds of the total production. But there was more to come from Metro, including a couple of extra doors in response to brand new rivals such as the Peugeot 205, Fiat Uno and Vauxhall Nova. The next big chapter in the Metro story would be 1984, but would history be rewritten?

Metro makes its appearance in style onboard the MS Vistafjord.

The cabaret style stage set-up for the Metro launch.

The MS *Vistafjord*, upon which the Metro dealer launch took place.

When it came to launching the Metro to its dealers, Leyland Cars pulled out all the stops to make sure the launch was as memorable as it could be.

But with a determination to keep the Metro's styling a secret until the October Motor Show, and the need to present the Metro to the dealer network at least a month in advance to allow them to place launch orders, the company was faced with a conundrum. How could it launch such a high-profile car away from prying eyes?

The answer was all at sea, literally. In a fascinating 2019 interview with aronline.co.uk, Austin-Morris's former Manager for Launch Planning and Special Events, Ken Clayton, explained, 'In the late 1970s most car manufacturers adopted a three-stage process to the launch of a new model. The first was to show it to the press, next in line came the dealers and fleet buyers – so they could get geared up to promoting and selling it – and the final stage was the public launch when the advertising programme swung into action. The Launch Planning and Special Events Department was responsible for the dealer and fleet parts of the launch sequence.

Planning for a launch generally took around six months or so. With the Metro it was different, because we all knew that it was a make or break car for the company. Get the Metro launch wrong and we could all pack up and go home. As a result, a great deal more effort went into all aspects of the event. For the dealer launches, we started the planning process in the summer of 1978, more than two years before the car was expected to make its public appearance.'

The idea of a cruise ship came about after a chance conversation between Ken and his boss, Tony Cumming, who had been involved in shooting a TV commercial aboard HMS *Ark Royal*, in which an off-the-cuff remark rapidly turned into a launch plan.

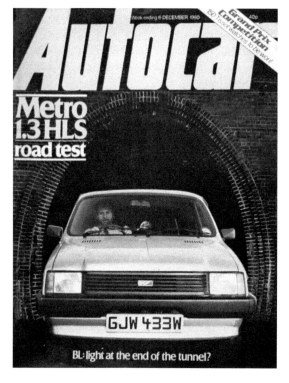

Autocar was highly complementary in early road tests.

Above: Inset headlamps were on base model and L.

Right: 5,000 miles in five days was a test enough for any car.

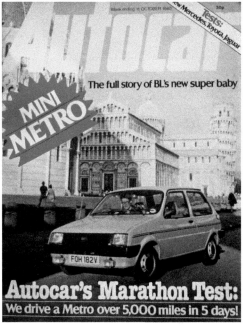

Four months later, Ken Clayton found himself in Puerto Rico choosing between two different ships that could be chartered and – critically – had enough room on their cabaret stages for a 'shock and awe' reveal of a new car.

The SS *Britanis* and the MS *Vistafjord* were the options, the latter being chosen for a sixteen-day programme at a cost of over £1.25 million, sailing out of Liverpool and with a drive programme on the Isle of Man, safely away from most of the British public.

Yet despite this, the media got hold of the information and very quickly the nationalised company's decision to spend a seven-figure sum on a cruise ship was making headline news.

'Ian Gronbach, a freelance journalist, had picked up on the fact that MS *Vistafjord* was calling in to Liverpool several times during September 1980,' Ken told aronline.co.uk.

I had taken a day off on 25 October and was driving home, listening to the evening news on BBC Radio. I was amazed to hear that the Metro launch was the lead story. The *Birmingham Evening Mail* followed and the next day, the *Daily Express, Birmingham Post, Daily Mail, Daily Telegraph, Sun, Mirror* and others ran the story. I don't know what effect this would have had in the office because it would have been dealt with by the PR Department (known as Product Affairs at the time) but they produced a brief for their team 'to be adhered to in answer to any queries about the [...] dealer launch trips.' The notes confirmed that 'BL Cars have chartered the cruise ship *Vistafjord* [...] to make a total of eight trips to the Isle of Man from Liverpool during the period 5 to 21 September.

They went on to explain that 'a total of 3200 guests have been invited [including] representatives of BL's 2000 sales outlets.' No costs were to be revealed but 'it is true to say that the cost is equivalent to holding a similar business function launching a major new car at a mainland venue.

Left: Standard mud flaps were removed for 1983.

Below: 'Anatomy of a World Beater'.

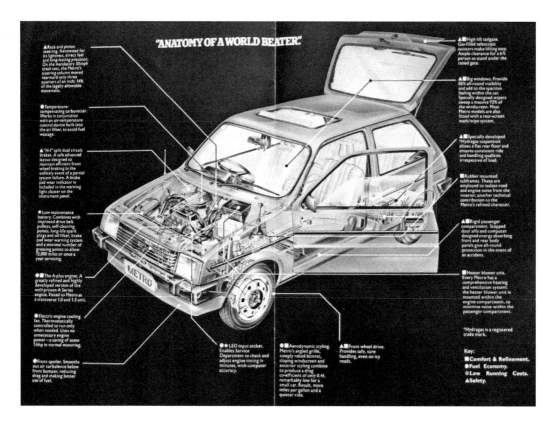

Former press and PR officer Ian Elliott remembers this episode well:

I still have a few mental scars from that! When the *Daily Mail* spotted the BL booking of the ship, there was a predictable 'Wasting Taxpayers' money story in the offing. I happened to be at Longbridge when it blew up, and it was suggested that I should break into Harold Musgrove's meeting with some vague idea that he might telephone the *Mail*'s Editor and get the story canned. Harold's Secretary was quite firm that was definitely not a good idea, and I wasn't minded to put my head in the Lion's mouth either. All we could do was standard damage limitation.

But what of the conference itself? Amid all the criticism, Ken and his team had plenty of planning to do.

Typically, this sort of event would start with the MD giving his state of the nation address and then we would go into a sequence of presentations dealing with the development of the new model, the reasons that it was superior to the competition, the market that it fitted into, the advertising to launch it along with much more,' Ken remembered. 'The whole thing culminated in the climactic moment which was the reveal of the new model. This was the first time the dealers would see the car in the metal and was designed to be as dramatic as possible and to show the new model off in the best possible way.

Some of the individual presentations were handled by senior directors and some were audio-visual sessions. Again, everything is different now but in 1980, we used a wide screen which was divided horizontally into three areas. A slide could be projected onto each area and all three butted up together. There were then two other screen areas covering the joins. It was known as 'two over three' and involved, in the case of Metro, a rack of 18 slide projectors and pre-recorded soundtracks. The whole thing was capable of presenting a continuous image across the screen which, when done well, was stunning. In the case of Metro, the business conference was on Day One while, on Day Two, there was the Metro launch after which the dealers were taken ashore to drive the car.

Automatic was launched as a standalone model, based on HLE.

Cutaway shows how Metro was brilliantly packaged.

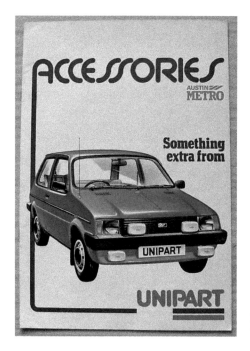

If you wanted to personalise your Metro, the Unipart accessory range was full of delights.

Three production companies, Caribiner, MMA and Roundel, pitched for this work, and in May 1980 Caribiner was chosen. The producer for Caribiner was David Lowe although he left well before the show took place. Kenny Neigh from Caribiner's New York office took over from him and he was joined by Gerry Pagliari and Julia Yesner, both also from New York. Jon Rollason, who had been a scriptwriter on the television soap *Crossroads*, was brought in as writer. In fact, Caribiner assembled an impressive team including Phil Grief as production manager, Gordon Roberts and Mollie Kirkland, a diminutive but hugely impressive show-caller.

'Over the next few months, I spent a lot of time working with this team and grew to respect their professionalism. But those months would prove to be amongst the most demanding and stressful of my working life,' Ken said.

Clayton joined the MS *Vistafjord* on 2 September by which time the supporting marquee areas where the dealers and fleet buyers would join the event were already in place. The cars and stage sets were also dockside, and the process of setting up the ship to accommodate the launch was not a small one. It would use an enormous floating crane named Mammoth and everything, including display cars, would be lifted onboard by it. It was at this point that the cars were scooped by a *Daily Mail* photographer.

Ken added:

On 5 September, rehearsals continued and, in the afternoon, the first group of dealers arrived. There were various difficulties with double-booked cabins for them and one dealer, who was told that he was in a double cabin with his wife, replied 'If you think I'm sharing a cabin with her, you've got another thing coming'.

That afternoon, at 5.00pm, we started the first performance of the Day One conference in front of a dealer audience. The computer controlling the slides had a glitch during one of the automated modules but, overall, the first show went well. At 10.00pm we had the cabaret

Launch accessories brochure shows
a host of personalisation options.

Above left: Not even the most robotised car in the UK was exempt from BL's strike actions.

Above right: A bold claim, maybe, but for once British Leyland was right.

which was a huge success and then, at 11.30pm, everything had to be re-set for the Day Two conference session. Overnight *MS Vistafjord* left Liverpool and relocated to Douglas on the Isle of Man. At 7.00am that morning, we started to get ready for the Day Two conference which included the reveal. The dealers loved it with most of them standing and applauding as the car appeared through the fog of dry ice to the soundtrack of *Land of Hope and Glory*.

The Leyland Princess

Perhaps the most famous person to buy a brand-new Metro in 1980 was Lady Diana Spencer, in the year before her marriage to Prince Charles.

The nineteen-year-old future Princess of Wales was living in an apartment in Earls Court at the time and worked in a nursery in Pimlico. After passing her driving test, she chose a new miniMetro as her first car and was regularly seen driving it to her work.

The car was a humble 1.0-litre model in Emberglow Red and was sold shortly after Charles and Diana got married (though not before Corgi Toys had jumped on the souvenir bandwagon with a Royal Wedding Metro), to be replaced by a Ford Escort XR3.

MPB 909W then went off the radar for a decade, before turning up at British Car Auctions in 1992, when the going rate for a twelve-year-old Metro was a mere three figures. Yet Princess Diana's car sold for £6,000 – around ten times its book value, and almost double its original purchase price.

It's worth a lot more than that today, however, and the car is currently one of the star exhibits at the Museum of Road Transport in Coventry, Warwickshire.

And the Winner Is...

Unsurprisingly, the Metro picked up a fair amount of silverware in its first full year on sale, even if it did go head-to-head with other significant new models such as the front-wheel-drive Ford Escort and the new Vauxhall Cavalier.

Among the gongs in the Longbridge trophy cabinet were the *What Car?* Best Small Car award, the Guild of Motoring Writers' 'Top Car' 1981, the RAC Dewar trophy for an outstanding British Car, the Duke of Edinburgh's Designer's Prize and the Don Safety Award.

But above all of these was the Design Council British Award – a real distinction. The judges said,

> The design shows the priority that was given to achieving 'big car' qualities in a compact, inexpensive vehicle. Excellent use of interior space, easy access, comfort and safety belong to a class of car larger than the Metro and combined with a low initial price, very good fuel economy and low operating and maintenance costs give outstanding value for money. The 'Mighty Metro' may well become a cult car like its predecessor, the Mini.

Trouble and Strife

Credit: Aronline.co.uk | Keith Adams

Much as the Metro was well-received, British Leyland was still a hotbed of industrial unrest, so it didn't take long for union strife to rear its ugly head.

Having narrowly avoided a strike over pay, BL found itself back in the headlines for all the wrong reasons. It all came to a head on 21 November 1980 and the cause was Metro seat production.

Discontent, which had rumbled among the 130 seat assemblers on the day shift for weeks, ended in a strike on the preceding Thursday. The management had pressed unsuccessfully for output to keep pace with the big demand for the new car and claimed that a few seat assemblers were refusing to work properly so that the day shift was achieving only 80 per cent of its target output, compared with the night shift's 98 per cent. It said the disparity between shifts with the same manning made nonsense of the day shift's claim that it required more workers. As a result, the Metro production line was stopped.

Angry groups of Metro workers stormed through the Longbridge plant, smashing windows and doors in protest at the management's stopping production of the new car. The plant was soon at a standstill. The trouble occurred when 500 assembly workers were laid off for the second time in a week because of the shortage of car seats.

Within minutes of the track being stopped, workmen began to storm through the plant, hurling car components through windows, knocking over racks of parts and terrifying female staff in adjoining offices.

One group of about thirty went to the 'Kremlin' (the management head office). When they found the doors locked, they ripped one from its hinges and forced their way into the office of Stanley Mullet, the Plant Director. They demanded and got a meeting with him, and other senior managers, to protest at the shutting down of the Metro line.

They were told that production would not resume until their colleagues began producing seats for the Metro in acceptable numbers. Several police cars were sent to the plant but did not enter. The difficulty over seats had been simmering for several weeks. With thousands of seatless Metros on the plant roads and more joining them daily, the management brought in outside suppliers, but workers refused to unload the seats they'd made.

Pickets said that the clash was simply a reflection of the widespread bad feeling resulting from the company's refusal to increase its 6.8 per cent wage offer. One picket said:

Today's trouble was always on the cards. It had brewed for weeks. For a time it was pretty hot in there with exhaust pipes and other parts from the racks flying all over the place. We are as proud of the Metro as any of the bosses, but they must learn they cannot keep riding roughshod over us.

Hundreds of other workers walked out in sympathy, stopping production of the Mini and the Allegro. As a result, several thousands more were sent home by management. BL said at the time:

We are still checking reports of damaged cars, but so far we have not been able to establish that anything significant happened in that respect. Talks are taking place with the works committee to try to resolve the problem but we have stated that the assembly line will not be restarted until the seat dispute is resolved.

The strike lasted two days and workers returned to a stockpile of 6,000 seatless Metros.

By mid-December 1980, BL was planning to recruit 1,000 extra workers to boost Metro production in preparation for its European launch.

CHAPTER 3

1984 – Facelift and Five-Door

A five-door version of the Metro had been proposed earlier on in the car's gestation but it never saw the light of day due to a lack of development funding (not helped by the emergency restyle) and the decision of BL's product planners that the market for a five-door supermini probably wasn't that great – after all, there were other, larger cars in the Leyland portfolio that catered for those who needed an extra set of doors.

But shortly after the Metro's introduction, there was a huge shift in the small hatchback market, with new European rivals coming along and advancing the sector. First to the market with five-doors was the 1981 Renault 5 'Cinque Portes', but behind it came the Peugeot 205 and Fiat Uno, both of which were mechanically simple but moved the game on in terms of packaging and interior design. The Metro was still popular, but it was no longer top of its class.

Furthermore, while customer feedback on the early Metros had been largely positive, one of the biggest criticisms from owners was that the cabin had a rather dated feel, with cheap parts-bin switchgear and a rather stark, utilitarian layout.

So with some strong sales and a clear opportunity to consolidate the Metro's market position by evolving it with the times, rather than behind them as had always been the BL way, the Metro saw some major changes ahead of its fifth year on sale.

It was needed, too. Ford had revamped the Fiesta in 1983 and the Fiesta Mk II had overtaken the Metro at the top of the sales charts, so Austin-Rover (as it now was after the

Metro facelift brought modernised looks and metric wheels.

sale of Jaguar and demise of Triumph and Morris) turned to its new chief stylist, Roy Axe, to freshen it up.

Axe had joined Austin-Rover from Chrysler – where he had designed the Alpine and Solara – at the end of 1982, after David Bache had fallen out with company boss Harold Musgrove and stormed out over delays to the upcoming Maestro. One of Axe's jobs was to set up a new design studio in Canley, Coventry, where a large amount of the company's corporate management was based.

While his primary remit was to work closely with Honda to develop domestic versions of the new cars planned under the new relationship between the two makers, most significantly the Rover 800 and new 200, the Metro facelift was his first project.

Metro was still a strong seller and its exterior styling was still highly contemporary, but there were criticisms over its old-fashioned steel bumpers and largely outdated cabin. Since its introduction, other cars had moved the game forward in interior design and there were significant cues from them in the restyled one-piece fascia, which was by far the most important change in the new Metro.

The instrument binnacle, for example, had a smart 'Matrix' pattern to it, similar to the Nissan Micra, while the one-piece dash moulding was contoured upwards around the dials, much like the Fiesta Mk II. There were improved seats, too, with firmer filling and thicker bolsters, along with a tilting mechanism that was far easier to reach. The seats were sturdier, but also thinner, increasing legroom for rear passengers.

Five-door was Austin-Rover's answer to European rivals.

METRO KILT TRE O CINQUE !

Italian market five-door launch model was the amusingly named Metro 'Kilt', with tartan seat covers.

External changes were minimal – a deeper front valance and a new one-piece radiator grille being the main changes, though the inset headlamps remained on more basic models. Low-spec cars also still kept their steel bumpers, but with wraparound plastic end caps to give the car a more modern appearance.

Higher up the range, a one-piece plastic bumper arrangement was introduced, which was either finished in grey or, on the MG and Vanden Plas (see separate chapter), body-coloured as was very much the trend in the industry at the time.

Another significant change was the switch to metric tyres, which were deemed to be the future. After all, tyre sizes across the world were a confusing mix of metric and imperial, and the car manufacturers were working to standardise them. The Metro got 150/65 315 TD tyres, which were about 12¾ inches, but despite the best efforts of some car manufacturers, the wheel and tyre manufacturers were so stubborn (no doubt because of the expense of new tooling) that the imperial/metric mix remains and metric tyres are – today – an expensive and specialist purchase. It's little surprise, then, that many of today's surviving Metros are rolling on aftermarket 13-inch alloys.

With the facelift came a change to the Metro's trim levels, with the entry-level 'base' Metro being referred to as the City, a name that had first appeared on the base Metro towards the end of pre-facelift production. The City was so basic that it didn't have reversing lamps, though a lamp holder and clear lens were still in the taillight moulding, requiring only bulbs and a reverse light switch to make them work. Early cars also only

Early facelift three-door features accessory foglamp grille.

Bonnet strakes aided cabin ventilation.

Above left: Austin Rover logo appeared behind Metro badging.

Above right: Facelift instrument binnacle had 'graphic' background.

got a driver's side sun visor, no parcel shelf and no provision for a radio. To add to the miserliness, there was no rear wash-wipe or heated window, and only one of the rear fog lamps contained a bulb.

The City really existed just so that Austin-Rover could advertise a £3,195 price point, with the volume entry model being the City X, just £300 more and with reversing lights, two sun visors, head restraints, a parcel shelf, front door bins, reclining rear seats, a rear wash-wipe and a heated rear window.

Move up to the Metro L and things got even more generous, with a choice of 1.0- or 1.3-litre engines, a choke warning light, push-button radio, a glovebox lid, armrests and a passenger door mirror, as well as twin coachlines to distinguish it from City models.

Next came the HLE, which got halogen headlamps aligned with the grille, side repeaters and side rubbing strips, plus internally adjustable door mirrors – a Metro first.

The rear parcel shelf was carpeted and as an extra touch of luxury the seatbelts were colour-keyed to match the upholstery, in either grey or beige. HLE was the top standard trim, with the MG and Vanden Plas variants offering even more spec.

Mechanically, the new Metros were largely the same as the early cars, but the hydraulic clutch was replaced by a simpler cable-operated mechanism that was not only cheaper, but also reduced the harsh drive uptake that had been a criticism of earlier models. There was sadly never the budget to develop a five-speed model, though, as there was no space within the A-Series 'gearbox in sump' arrangement to accommodate the additional ratio.

Later in 1984, at the British Motor Show, Austin-Rover revealed its most significant new Metro since launch. The new five-door was part of the product plan from the start, but with no budget left to continue development, the idea was put on a backburner. But with an extra pair of doors, not only could Metro compete with the Peugeot 205, Fiat Uno and Renault 5, but it also had enough ammunition to once again climb to the top of the UK sales charts, leapfrogging the Fiesta that had knocked it off its perch.

And there it would remain through 1985 and 1986, eventually being surpassed by the Ford Escort as buyers started to favour slightly larger cars. In 1986, the millionth Metro rolled off the production line – a silver Vanden Plas that was given away as a competition prize on the 'Wogan' television show.

Despite being second in the market, the Metro remained a strong seller. As the supermini market evolved, so did the Metro. The entry-level City was made less miserly, and the range also followed the 1980s trend of special edition models being offered, with such gems as the Metro Principles, named after the high street fashion chain and featuring white hubcaps, and the Metro Moritz, a glorified ski-themed City X with special decals and silver paint.

In 1986, the Metro Mayfair was added to the line-up, with plush velour trim and most of the specification of the Vanden Plas, including optional electric windows, but no wood trim. It was perfect Middle England fodder, and became one of the range's best-sellers as a rival to the Ford Fiesta Ghia.

All the while, backroom negotiations were going on at Austin-Rover. Following the launch of the Rover 800, the marketing team were keen to push the brands upmarket. It was apparent at boardroom level that it was time for Austin-Rover to return to private ownership and the stumbling block was the awkward historical connotations of the marques. By 1986, only Austin, MG, Vanden Plas, Rover and Land Rover remained, and it was deemed internally that Austin was tarnished with the reputation of models such as the Allegro and Maxi, which were synonymous with industrial unrest and poor quality.

To prepare Austin-Rover for sale, the Austin name was dropped in late 1987 and the company was renamed 'Rover Group', with the flagship models retaining the Rover name. At the same time, there was a bid from General Motors to buy Land Rover, which ultimately failed, but showed that a brand with Rover in its name was still a marketable proposition. Indeed, it was Land Rover that would go on to keep the company afloat in the next decade, but that's a story that comes later.

In late 1987, ahead of the proposed sale, the Rover brand was kept for the SD3 (200) and 800 saloons, but the Austin name was dropped from all of the other models, with MG and Vanden Plas retaining their identities, and the other cars becoming Mini, Metro, Maestro and Montego in their own right. In their current form, they weren't considered 'good enough' to be Rovers, though the Metro would redress this later, unlike its larger siblings.

By 1988, Rover Group was no longer in public ownership, nine years after it had been acquired by the government in an emergency rescue package. Instead, it had been sold wholesale to another previously nationalised company – British Aerospace. A new chapter in Rover's history, and Metro's, was about to begin...

Mugs, key rings and even a sports bag; for the Metro owner who has everything.

CHAPTER 4

1988 – The British Aerospace Years

In 1986, the then Prime Minister, Margaret Thatcher, appointed Canadian businessman Graham Day to the role of Chairman and Managing Director of Austin-Rover. His role, first and foremost, was to prepare the company for sale and return it to private ownership, as had been her remit with many of the UK's nationalised companies including British Gas, British Telecom, British Steel and North Sea Oil.

First, Day divested the company of its commercial vehicle and bus manufacturing operations, with Leyland trucks being acquired by Dutch HGV company DAF and the bus operation sold to a conglomeration of body manufacturers that had previously worked with Leyland, including Alexander, Dennis and Optare (which still has the famous Leyland 'plughole of doom' displayed outside its Sherburn-in-Elmet headquarters in West Yorkshire).

CAR's interview with Graham Day gave many clues to the future, unlike its artists' impressions.

Following the demise of Austin, Metro became a standalone name.

New trims were introduced, including Sport, GS and Mayfair.

Next to go was the van division, with DAF again being the primary investor. Leyland-DAF Vans, or LDV, would continue to produce variants of the Sherpa, based on the chassis of the 1959 Austin Cambridge/Morris Oxford, until 2005.

That left Austin, Rover and Land Rover. Land Rover, after an ill-fated sales pitch to General Motors, was given a new remit to take on the Japanese manufacturers, which it manifested to great success with the Discovery and – later – the Freelander. Rover, meanwhile, had its hopes invested in the new 'R8' 200, which would see the brand reach mainstream territory.

The elephant in the room was Austin. Rover Group needed fleet volume which, until the new Rover product line-up was complete, fell on the shoulders of Metro, Maestro and Montego, with the Mini continuing to plough its own cultish furrow well after its original sell-by date.

If anything, Rover Group was embarrassed by the Maestro and Montego. Underdeveloped, under-evolved and antiquated, they would stand in the way of the company's future plans. But the Metro was different. It was still the company's best-selling model, but the funding the government had committed to Rover Group's future was aimed at its future model portfolio, and that meant that all available funds were directed towards the R8/200 project.

The Metro, meanwhile, would need to stand alone and continue to generate sales, something it had to do as a brand of its own. Within the forward plan was a development of Metro to bring it up to date, but in the lead-up to the R8 launch it fell to the marketing department to promote and evolve the existing car, which it did with surprising success.

This is a late Metro Clubman from 1990; by then, the badge was shaped like a Rover shield, but it still wasn't called a Rover.

Late Metro GS was one of the plusher models.

Sporty ARX was one of the more unusual special editions.

So as Austin-Rover disappeared, a new Metro line-up emerged, largely the same as the existing model range, but with a renewed focus on retail sales from a myriad of special editions and some new hero models, including the GTa, which was effectively an MG Metro but without the tuning elements.

The GTa came with multi-spoke alloy wheels, body-coloured trim, sports seats, a four-speaker stereo and side skirts and was, in many ways, the first iteration of a 'warm' hatch, with hot hatch looks and a more tepid engine.

The range evolved to include the far better-equipped City and City X, the Clubman (replacing the L) the plush GS, the Sport, the even plusher Mayfair and the existing MG and Vanden Plas.

But the main focus for retail sales was on 'Special Editions', a fad that ran deep in the late eighties across all manufacturers and which saw more Metro variants than ever before. It's impossible to list them all here, not least because overseas markets created many of their own, and others were dealer specials such as the Metro GMX, which were only sold in Manchester and surrounding areas. But the main protagonists included the ARX, Advantage, Chelsea, Red Hot, Jet Black, Studio 2, Mosaic and Sprite (among many others). It would be a strategy that would also see the next generation Metro through the 1990s, as car manufacturers battled to increase market share.

But as the special editions evolved, so did the UK car market, and it soon became apparent that the Metro was rapidly approaching its sell-by date. Slowing sales, a lack of five-speed transmission and compromised packaging meant the Metro was falling behind as other European and Japanese manufacturers upped their game.

Red Hot was Jet Black's twin.

Metro Clubman continued as an automatic until 1992.

CHAPTER 5

AR6 – The Ill-Fated Replacement

Plans to replace the Metro began as early as 1984, when the model was still selling strongly and had just received its facelift.

With £1.5 billion of government investment towards the project and a new design studio headed up by Roy Axe, three models were tabled that would ultimately not see the light of day, codenamed AR5, AR6 and AR7.

The AR5 was a reskin of the 'SD3' Rover 213/216 but was shelved early on as development of the R8 200 began apace, while AR7 was a rebodied Maestro which again was shelved in order to make way for the R8.

AR6, however, was a supermini designed to take on the bold new European designs such as the Peugeot 205 and Fiat Uno and was both wider and longer than the Metro. A number of design proposals were put forward – one styled by Axe himself and the other, nicknamed 'The Mouse', was penned by stylists Stephen Harper and David Saddington, both of whom had been brought into the design team by Roy Axe.

The latter design was more of a 'monobox' style and was very quickly killed off by senior management. It's a fascinating and space-efficient design that would still look contemporary today and has to be one of Austin-Rover's biggest missed opportunities.

The early AR6 prototype had mock-up 1984 number plates, suggesting that was its release date. (AROnline)

Clay mock-up sits on MG Metro wheels. (AROnline)

AR6X study was smaller and more of a city car.

The second AR6 proposal, Roy Axe's design, featured a number of the designer's trademark styling cues, such as a large glass area and a floating roofline, which did away with the need for thick body-coloured pillars and would become a styling feature of both the 800 and the R8.

It was to be a hugely advanced car with an all-aluminium bodyshell to reduce weight and improve fuel economy, as well as one that would be highly aerodynamic and have class-leading safety features, many of which had been trialled on the ECV3 concept in 1983.

An all-new three-cylinder engine was planned, too, alongside a new four-cylinder and a number of spin-off models, with a convertible (which would supposedly be badged as the MG Midget) and a coupe, similar in concept to the Honda CRX.

But as always, budget pressures forced a number of rethinks. There was government funding incoming, but the Maestro and Montego weren't the sales success that Austin-Rover had hoped for and the profit that the two models were supposed to generate simply didn't exist. That resulted in changes, including a rationalisation of the range.

Speaking to *AROnline* in 2017, Harold Musgrove said, 'By 1985, it was a steel-bodied car in three- and five-door forms, with further derivatives planned. You have to design the derivatives from the outset.

Wheel spats were designed to reduce aerodynamic resistance. (AROnline)

Ribbed rear lamps were one styling treatment considered. (AROnline)

Rakish lines and 'floating' roof were Roy Axe styling cues. (AROnline)

There would be no three-cylinder version, due to the increased weight of the all steel bodyshell.'

The derivatives were dropped, too, but development of AR6 continued, with a number of running prototypes developed for testing ahead of a planned on-sale date of 1988.

The project was stalled further, though, after a torrid sales year in 1985, where Austin-Rover sales slumped by 20 per cent in the face of Japanese and European imports, as well as strong fleet performances from Ford and Vauxhall.

As a result, the government accelerated its plans to privatise the company and entered into negotiations with Ford, which came very close to fruition. However, the sale never happened for political reasons and Austin-Rover was left to face its own problems. There were some sweeping changes at the top, with Harold Musgrove being replaced by Graham Day, who was appointed with a remit of preparing the company for sale by the then Prime Minister, Margaret Thatcher.

One of the first decisions Day made was to kill off the AR6 programme altogether; an unprecedented move for a model so far down the development path, but a decision that was considered essential in order to nurture Austin-Rover's relationship with Honda, described by Day as 'the only part of the company worth a damn'.

The demise of AR6 was considered a travesty by many within the company, who believed that its advanced design and excellent packaging would have made it an instant best-seller and been enough to return Austin-Rover to profitability, but aside from the development of a new engine – the upcoming K-Series – nothing from the AR6 was carried forward. It was stillborn and is believed by many to be Austin-Rover's biggest missed opportunity of all time.

But what of the Metro, now its replacement was dead in the water? After the sale of Austin-Rover to British Aerospace in 1987, a 'new' Metro was high on the list of priorities for Rover Group. But with no money being generated from the rest of the model range, it would need to be done quickly and make use of a lot of existing architecture. Enter 'R6', the 1990 Rover Metro...

Vertical rear lamps and narrow pillars would still look modern today. (AROnline)

CHAPTER 6

1990 – A New Metro for the 1990s

With the AR6 cull came a decision from Rover Group management to press ahead with the development of a heavily revised Metro, codenamed R6.

Due to cost constraints, there wasn't the budget for Rover to develop an entirely new car and the development of R6 was soured by the feelings of many in the engineering team over the decision not to progress with AR6, but by late 1987 there were two designs on the table – the R6 and the R6X. The first was a reskinned Metro using the same bodyshell and the R6X was a more adventurous proposal, based on the same platform but with a new body altogether.

The original plan was to develop both, but R6X was quickly killed off on cost grounds. The R6, however, was full-speed ahead in its development, and although it necessitated the use of the Metro shell, glass and chassis, it would still get the new K-Series engine and end-on Peugeot-sourced gearbox, which would require revisions to the engine bay and bulkhead.

There was also a need to revisit the Metro's suspension system. Although the ride and handling of the original Metro were considered good for their time, a lot had changed in the 1980s, and cars such as the exceptional Peugeot 205 and later Citroen AX had proven

A new Metro for a new decade, and Rover was very proud of it.

redesigned | re-engineered

New-look front end gave Metro a modern appearance despite its aged body shell.

Even basic cabins were well-finished.

that small cars could be made to grip and handle terrifically. What Rover needed was a sharper set-up that retained the Metro's impressive ride but balanced it out with a degree of handling sophistication.

The favoured solution was to go with a conventional front strut and rear trailing arm set-up, as had been the plan for AR6. But it soon became apparent that to incorporate such changes would not only require a lot of tooling investment but would also compromise the Metro's cabin space and luggage capacity, which were already behind the class due to the model's compact dimensions.

Plan B, then, was to refine the existing Hydragas set-up and give the car a slightly wider track, that would balance off its handling, as well as fit new 13-inch wheels and dispense with the awkward metric ones that were fitted to the existing Metro.

There were also plans to change the bulkhead, to lower the steering wheel to a more conventional position and to lengthen the nose of the car, bring the front axle forward and give more legroom for front passengers.

Even then, though, the Hydragas set-up made the Metro wallowy and less agile to drive than some of its European rivals.

The answer came from Dr Alex Moulton, the man who had invented both Hydrolastic and Hydragas suspension systems in the first place and who had outspokenly campaigned for the Metro to have front-to-rear interconnected Hydragas at launch – a decision ruled out by BL's product chief Spen King, on the basis of cost. Undeterred, Moulton bought himself a Metro HLE and modified it himself to demonstrate the effectiveness of an interconnected system, inviting *CAR Magazine* to come and drive it and deliver a verdict on its virtues.

Later that same year, Moulton invited former Leyland boss Michael Edwardes to his house for a social meeting, during the course of which he took Edwardes out in his car. Having driven the Moulton Metro, Edwardes is said to have picked up the phone to Graham Day and told him he needed to integrate it into R6. Day invited Moulton to bring his car to Canley and assembled a team of chassis engineers to drive it, all of whom agreed it was a major advance over the original Metro set-up. The answer, it seemed, had been staring them in the face all along.

While decisions were being made about the suspension, the styling team had been busy creating a modern nose and stylish rear lights for the new car, while the new dashboard and cabin were also getting signed off. Given the parameters they had to work from, they achieved a masterpiece, with a smart and quality feeling interior that was plusher than most of its supermini rivals, even if space in the rear was a bit cramped.

The first production specification prototypes hit the road in late 1988, with a target launch date of early 1990. The attentions of the company's management then turned to how the Metro would be marketed.

8v K-Series engine brought Metro to life.

Higher spec cars got a rev counter and chunky steering wheel.

A large part of this was internal debate about the name. The 'brandless' Metro, Maestro and Montego models from the 1988 model year onward were Austin nameplates, and the demise of the old brand still had strong connotations with Metro, so there was some debate about whether or not to change the name. There were others inside the company who were reticent to calling it a Rover; after all, the smallest Rover to date was the 213, and that had upset the purists.

For a long while, it looked like 'Rover 100' would be the overarching model name, as this sat well with the 800 and newly introduced 200 'R8', but Rover Metro was still a strong contender, as was the rather contrived 'Metro – by Rover'. However, dealers were very keen to retain the Metro nameplate as it resonated well with existing customers, so the decision was taken to sell the car as the Rover Metro in the UK only, and as the Rover 100-Series in export markets.

The Metro made its debut in May 1990 at a time when Rover was, for the first time in living memory, riding the crest of a wave. The 200 had debuted seven months earlier and was hugely praised for its impressive ride and handling, as well as the performance of its new 1.4-litre K-Series engine.

For the Metro, the K-Series was adapted further, with single cam versions of the unit in 1.4 and all-new 1.1-litre guise, developing either 75 bhp or 60 bhp. For the first time, Metro could also be ordered with a five-speed transmission, though a four-speeder was standard on lower trim levels.

S and Si spec got red side stripes and seat belts.

On higher specs mirrors and bonnet vents were colour keyed.

Trim levels were the rudimentary Metro C, the mass-market L, the vaguely sporty S and Si, the sportier GTa and the range topping GTi 16v. The Vanden Plas and Mayfair names were consigned to the history books. It was a much more youthful line-up in terms of both styling and marketing, and although the roots of the car were evident in its bodyshell and small glass area, the changes were sufficient for it to achieve a rapturous reception from the automotive media, who, it seemed, were really willing the revitalised Rover Group to succeed. Plus, the changes to the car's performance, ride and handling as a result of the new suspension set up were boldly evident.

The car certainly won over *What Car?* which said:

> The New Metro is a quantum leap, and on several accounts. For a start it's light years ahead of its predecessor, far more so than its obvious family resemblance would suggest. But, more important still, it sets new standards of quality, ride and refinement for the class. In its chassis dynamics – ride and handling – it takes on the acknowledged masters of the art, the French, and beats them. It's probably the quietest, smoothest, most refined car this side of £10,000 or even a bit higher.
>
> Drive the Metro, and unless you need more space you wonder if you need anything grander. Our only reservation concerns the fuel economy, which really ought to be better.

Such high praise was matched by *Autocar*, which enthused: 'This is our new British hero'.

Rover marketed the Metro as a completely new car, glossing over the fact it was essentially a heavily facelifted ten-year-old design. It used the catchphrase 'metromorphosis' in its marketing and followed it up with 'the New Metro, with Rover Engineering', playing the Rover card for all it was worth.

And it worked. While some within the company were sceptical about the Metro's sales potential, the car even caught Rover's internal forecasters by surprise, leading to a waiting list for the first nine months of production – astonishing considering the story behind the car's gestation.

There were gaps in the range, though. No automatic, which meant that the old Metro carried on for another eighteen months for those who needed a self-shifting transmission,

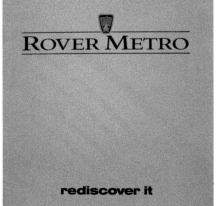

Above left: Metro R6 came with a range of new colours.

Above right: 'Rediscover it' – Rover invited buyers to revisit Metro.

and a lack of a diesel left the range behind some of its rivals in the market, notably the Ford Fiesta, with which it constantly jostled for market share.

But, essentially, the new Metro was an overwhelming success, and with the 200 and new 400 saloon going great guns, Rover suddenly found itself in a purple patch. Could the decision to privatise the company have been a greater success than anyone gave it credit for, and was the decision to kill off the AR6 not such a bad idea after all? In 1990, it certainly seemed so. Even more so when the new Metro was awarded the 1991 Car of the Year award by *What Car?*

Initial sales kept the Metro right near the top of sales charts and in May 1992 an automatic model finally arrived, using a CVT gearbox developed in-house by Rover and

Above: The suggestion that the Metro diesel was refined and quiet was perhaps a claim too far.

Left: Dynamics were much improved thanks to interconnected Hydragas.

fitted to 1.4-litre models. The transmission was a major development, as not only would it replace the antiquated Mini-sourced transmission from the old Metro, but it would also give Rover an auto they could use on its own future models, including the new 200, which was due to appear in a couple of years' time. At the time, CVT was all the rage in small autos, with Ford, Fiat and later Nissan all using continuously variable systems in their small autos.

The Metro range was finally completed in January 1993 with the use of PSA's TUD diesel engine under licence, the 1,360cc engine being the same as used in the Peugeot 106 and Citroen AX. Its 52 bhp output was nothing to write home about, but 78 mpg at 56 mph was, and the 1.4d became the most economical Metro ever made. It was rather sluggish and agricultural, but for some buyers, the economy benefits were enough.

But those strong initial sales weren't sustained, not least because by 1993 the supermini market had moved on substantially. The Ford Fiesta was a much more modern design from the outset, but was hardly sharp to drive, yet it still led the market. However, it was a vintage year for superminis with the new bubbly Vauxhall Corsa, even rounder British-built Nissan Micra K11 and sharply styled and brilliantly packaged Fiat Punto new on the market. Shortly after the Metro's launch, Renault had brought sophistication to the supermini sector in the shape of the Clio. It was both a crowded and highly competitive market, with cut-throat margins and manufacturers constantly reducing their own profitability in pursuit of market share.

In 1993, for example, Rover sold 57,068 Metros in the UK, compared to Ford's 110,449 Fiestas, and more than 20,000 units behind the Metro's performance in 1990, when over 81,000 were sold. As with the previous model, Rover started punting out all the special editions it could think of to shore-up sales, with names such as Quest, Rio, Rio Grande, Nightfire, Tahiti, Casino Royale and even a '57', which was produced for a competition by food company Heinz.

Diesel engine had 'TU' on the engine cover, a nod to PSA.

Launch spec Rover Metro with boats in the background but it wasn't a tow car.

If you're looking for a no compromise small car – the sort of car that prompted What Car? to say 'No other small car rides as well or handles so neatly', then the two new Metro special editions, Quest and Quest Plus, offer unrivalled value for money. Both cars feature the award winning 1.1 litre K-Series engine

Quest PLUS PLUS EDITION

£6,995

offering responsive performance and economical motoring. Combined with outstanding suspension, they offer the kind of ride comfort you normally find only in larger cars.

Added to which Metro Quest and Quest Plus provide an impressive list of features.

Metro Quest specification includes

full width wheel trims, special Quest badge, colour co-ordinated interior and passenger door mirror, at the very sensible price of £5,995.

The Quest Plus is even more impressive.

Features include a rear wash-wipe (with intermittent wiper), an electronic tune 3 band stereo radio/cassette

Quest EDITION

£5,995

with Autostore, and two speakers. There's also a digital clock, a 60/40 split rear seat and tasteful pastels design interior trim.

And for this attractive package you pay a very attractive price £5,995.

Quest was one of the more basic Metro special editions.

But the poor sales performance was a conundrum that led to substantial infighting with Rover Group. The new 'R3' 200 was in advanced stages of development and was smaller than the R8. That car's proper replacement was the HH-R, the last Rover to be jointly developed with Honda and one that would go on to cause major headaches at boardroom level in 1994, when BMW gazumped Honda to buy the company after negotiations with the Japanese manufacturer were at an advanced stage.

The original plan was to introduce 200 as the Metro replacement and to launch 400 as the R8 successor, the rationale being that the 200 would be a large supermini that would take conquest sales from the class above despite a higher price point. It was an interesting idea and one that may well have worked if history had turned out differently, but in 1994 one of the most unexpected and divisive announcements in the car industry sent shockwaves through Longbridge.

Having successfully rebuilt Rover's reputation and market share, but having failed to address the profitability issues, British Aerospace had been trying for a while to find a buyer. Relations with Honda had reaped rewards for both companies, with Rover learning lots about efficient manufacturing and initial build quality, while the Japanese firm got the benefit of some great chassis engineering and design expertise that helped it develop cars that were both classier and more dynamic than Japanese rivals. It was also about to open its brand-new plant in Swindon and the synergies of a more advanced partnership, including majority ownership of Rover were evident.

Indeed, the 1993 Rover 600 and 1994 400 'HH-R' saw a return to Honda leading the joint project designs, with Rover's remit being to develop the smaller 200 and a replacement for the 800 executive saloon, which would never materialise in the form planned at the time.

But with Honda negotiations at the 'i' dotting and 't' crossing stage, BMW made a late bid for the company, a combination of an Anglophile boss, Bernd Pischetsrieder, and a desire to learn more about SUV expertise from Land Rover being the primary appeal. BMW brought with it some clear investment; a budget to develop a proper compact executive car, a desire to finally replace the ancient Mini with a new generation and a reputation for impeccable build quality. The eleventh-hour purchase surprised the entire car industry, none more so than at Honda, where relationships were soured so much that Honda would make it impossible for Rover to ever make a profit out of the HH-R project, which was its volume fleet seller. By ramping up the cost of bodyshells and dashboard mouldings throughout the car's life, Honda made the 400 and subsequent 45 a thorn in Rover's side until the bitter end.

This also had a major impact on Metro. Aware of the challenges that HH-R was to bring and with BMW focusing its efforts on the new 'R50' Mini and 'R40' Rover 700 (later the 75), it was decided to reposition the new 200 away from being a large supermini and towards being a compact 'C-Sector' car that would compete with the likes of the Ford Escort and Vauxhall Astra. By doing so, the car could be priced higher, so the original plan to launch it with a 1.1-litre engine was shelved, along with the more basic trim levels. Instead, engines would range from a 1.4 8v unit up to a 1.8 VVC, with some rather bold pricing to boot.

HH-R, meanwhile, would also be ambitiously priced in order to redress the costs of producing it in the first place, and would be marketed as a rival to the Ford Mondeo and

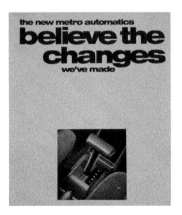 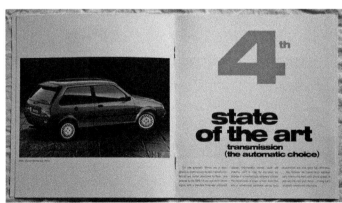

Above left: New CVT gearbox was developed specifically for the Metro.

Above right: At the time, CVT was all the rage.

Vauxhall Cavalier; something that led Rover into ploughing its own furrow with a saloon model, though the Honda-designed Civic Aerodeck would never be licensed to Rover, forcing the R8-based 400 Tourer to continue well beyond its sell-by date to keep options open for fleet buyers.

That left a sizeable gap between Mini and 200, and a very old car sitting in it. By 1995, even though it had been rapturously received five years earlier, Metro was positively archaic compared to most of its rivals and there was no money in the pot to replace it yet. In BMW's eyes that replacement would be the Mini, but there was no way it would see the light of day before the end of the century.

The Metro – already a fourteen-year-old design – was about to be thrown another lifeline...

Three-door models had a higher fuel filler for convenience and better safety.

By the mid-1990s, though, Metro was past its sell-by date, but it wasn't the end.

Alex Moulton's Metro was used to demonstrate the benefits of interconnected Hydragas.

CHAPTER 7

Goodbye Metro – Hello 100

With Metro sales in freefall and the new Mini in a frenzy of development, the only option available to Rover was to give the Metro yet another rework.

There were many in the company against the idea, but in order to launch the 200 as a 'premium' model, there needed to be a model below it to justify the brand positioning as well as to support Rover Group's fleet department, which needed to service the requirements of multi-user fleets who required superminis as much as large cars, the daily rental sector being one of the most important.

100 was hastily conceived, front end styling was from a 200 design study.

Three-spoke wheel helped modernise cabin.

Plus, its retail network still needed a supermini, for although almost every one of the Metro's rivals was now a more beguiling proposition, there was still an astonishing amount of patriotism and loyalty allied to the British brand. And while many of those buyers were older citizens, this was good news for the dealer network as their allegiance to Rover would mean they'd be unlikely to explore the other options in the class and would often pay list price, from savings rather than finance.

The decision to launch the new Rover 100 in 1995 was clearly a commercial-led one rather than product-led. It appeared in January 1995 and – unlike the metamorphosis from A-Series Metro to K-Series – it was a rushed and somewhat half-baked attempt.

The front end was different: the beaked nose and curvy headlights lifted directly from an early R3 200 styling study, which had been the design team's second choice for the larger car's new look.

Inside the dashboard was essentially unchanged, while the seats were the same carryover ones that the Rover Metro had borrowed from the Rover 200 'R8', though this was no bad thing as they were extremely supportive and comfortable.

There were new seat fabrics, though, in rather flamboyant 'Paisley' designs, along with a chunkier three-spoke steering wheel that had a more rounded central boss, which did a surprising amount to modernise the cabin.

Trim levels were i, Si, Sli, GSi and GTa, though a GTi version of the 100 would never materialise as Rover realised the car was no longer an appealing prospect for younger

Wood trim and Paisley door cards mark this out as a GSi.

Rear lamp lenses were the same shape as Metro but with smoked finish.

Fuel injection was standard across the 100 range.

GSi had genuine wood inserts.

Knightsbridge was the poshest later model.

buyers and that the car's traditional customers would favour luxury over sportiness. Indeed, the GSi in particular was supremely well-equipped, much more so than most cars at its price point and was even fitted with a wood-capped dashboard.

Engines were carried over, too, although the 16v 1.4 was dropped and the diesel replaced by PSA's slightly larger 64 bhp TUD.

The model names were 111 (for the 1.1-litre K-Series), 114 (for the 75 bhp 1.4) and 115d for diesel models.

It sold in steadily declining numbers through 1995 and 1996, but with the Mini development continuing apace, optimism was still within Rover Group that it would retain enough market share in the supermini sector for Rover to keep it going until the new car's appearance.

In 1997, a decision across Rover Group to drop the last two letters of each model name led to all cars being badged as simply '100', in line with the 200, 400, 600 and 800 series, which also got the new nomenclature. But unlike the larger cars, where a they would still be referred to in the price lists as a 200 216GSi or a 400 414SLi, the 100 range was changed again, with the model's names being taken – randomly – from areas of London and the South East. The base spec car became known as the 100 Ascot, the next model up was the Kensington, and above that came the Knightsbridge, with the GTa and GSi continuing as the range-toppers. There was more Paisley added to the interior, too, along with ribbed velour on plusher models, which took their seats from the facelifted HH-R.

The rejuvenated range actually saw an upturn in sales in 1997, though this was more likely down to heavy discounting and an upturn in the British economy than any increased desire for the car, which was still great fun to drive and well-appointed, but way below class standards.

Then, in October 1997, Rover was hit in the face by a concrete block. Quite literally.

It was around this time that the European New Car Assessment Programme (Euro NCAP) began as a means of testing both the passive and active safety of new cars; passive safety being their protection in an impact and active safety being their means of avoiding one in the first place.

Kensington was mid-range trim.

Layout was simple but by late 1990s standards the cabin was boxy and cramped.

In the UK, it was the Transport Research Laboratory (TRL) in Thatcham, Berkshire, that won the contract to crash test a number of vehicles in the Euro NCAP programme, one of which was the Rover 100.

Not only did the 100 achieve just one out of five stars for passive safety, with optional ABS being the only crash avoidance system it could muster, but it also scored just one star in the offset crash test, with the dummy in the driver's seat acquiring injuries that would have been 'almost certainly fatal' in a 30 mph impact. The chilling footage, which showed the car folding up in the middle and the crash test dummy smacking into the windscreen pillar, was a PR disaster for Rover Group.

TRL said it 'fell a long way behind what was considered a minimum standard in passive with a similarly disastrous showing in side impact tests, where the point of impact pushed the car's door straight into the dummy's upper thigh'. Unfortunately for Rover, this story became a lot more widespread than the specialist press and it transcended the usual car magazines into the daily newspapers. If that wasn't bad enough, the day after the results were revealed, footage of the crash test was broadcast on the BBC evening news and Rover's press department was inundated with angry phone calls.

In fairness, the 100 was essentially a seventeen-year-old design by this point and its performance was being compared to that of brand-new cars, but there was no way for Rover to fend off the flak. The 100's reputation had been indelibly tarnished, and it spelt the end for a car on which the hopes and dreams of Britain's car industry had once so stridently rode.

On 31 December 1997, the very last Rover 100 rolled off the production line – a silver 100 GSi, signed by all of those who helped build it. The car still exists and resides at the

Rover's paint finishes were exceptional. This was Amaranth Micatallic.

And this was Kingfisher Blue.

British Motor Museum in Gaydon, Warks, as a lasting reminder of the British car that was originally there to beat the world, but ultimately became a victim of its own longevity. A rather ignominious end for a car that had once been so well loved.

It wasn't until late 1998 that the 100 disappeared from Rover dealerships, though, with dealers struggling to shift the residual stock after the Euro NCAP debacle. The Mini, meanwhile, was still not ready, so Rover had introduced a new basic version of the 200 – the 211i – as a Metro for the new Millennium, a move that many argued should have happened in 1995.

Horrific Euro NCAP crash test result sounded final death knell for 100.

Final 100s were produced in December 1997.

CHAPTER 8

Replacing Metro – The 211 and CityRover

With the 100 no longer viable and a clear need to service the demands of customers who still wanted a small Rover, the company looked back to its original plans for the model's eventual replacement.

Back before the arrival of BMW, the 1995 'R3' 200 was pitched as the Metro replacement, but when the model was repositioned upwards, the proposed entry-level car using a 60 bhp 1.1-litre K-Series engine was dropped.

THE ROVER 211i

Above: 211 was originally planned as Metro replacement.

Right: Trim was basic with 60 bhp 8v engine.

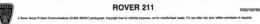

ROVER 211

However, a lot of the development work had already been done and by late 1998, just eight months after the 100 ceased production, Rover launched the '211' variant of the 200, with a fuel-injected version of the Metro's 1.1-litre powerplant.

It was originally sold in just two trim levels – the 211i and 211SE, which got electric front windows and ABS. The car was a surprise success for Rover, and by the time the 200 evolved into the 25 two years later, it accounted for around 15 per cent of sales, leading Rover to increase the number of trim levels available for its replacement.

By 2003 though, MG Rover Group was in dire need of support, with an aged product range and several ongoing bids for partnerships and external investment. One of those partnerships was with Indian carmaker Tata, which had won European type approval for its Indica supermini. At the same time, Rover dealers were crying out for a 'New Metro', so a deal was struck. Rover would import the Indica and modify it in the UK, the process of 'Roverisation' to include a new grille, steering wheel and stereo fascia plus 'CityRover' badging on the tailgate to reflect the chosen model name.

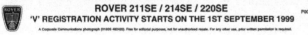

ROVER 211SE / 214SE / 220SE
'V' REGISTRATION ACTIVITY STARTS ON THE 1ST SEPTEMBER 1999

211, 214 and 220SE looked outwardly identical.

ROVER 25 1.1i / 1.1iE

25 1.1 replaced 211 in 2000.

While it was actually quite good fun to drive, with a lively engine that could – ironically – trace its roots back to the original Metro's former nemesis, the Peugeot 205, the CityRover was dreadfully finished with horrid interior plastics. It was a far cry from what Rover once stood for as a brand and its case wasn't helped by the company refusing to lend out a press car to *BBC Top Gear*, which borrowed one from a dealer instead, with predictably disastrous results.

Nevertheless, the CityRover demonstrated that there was still a fairly strong level of brand loyalty towards Rover in its home market, with over 10,000 sold in just over two years. A long way behind Metro's heyday, but a surprising number of buyers for such an inferior car, heavy discounting or not.

Above left: CityRover was Rover's new supermini for 2003.

Above right: Styling was by Giuigiaro and based on Tata Indica.

Right: The interior looked okay, but build quality was poor.

CHAPTER 9

The Metro Vanden Plas

One of the more unusual brands to survive the Michael Edwardes cull was Vanden Plas, the name of a once luxurious coachmaker that was eventually hoovered up by BMC and subsequently British Leyland.

During that time, Vanden Plas had evolved from building glorious Rolls-Royce powered luxury saloons to the rather ignominious position of nailing chrome grilles and picnic tables onto Austin Allegros at its Kingsbury Works in North-West London. Kingsbury itself had shut down in 1979, but Allegro VPs remained on sale until 1981 finished at Longbridge.

The future for Vanden Plas, though, would be as a trim level for Leyland's top-spec cars, with the first iterations being high-spec variants of the Rover SD1 and Austin Ambassador in 1981, as well as V12-engined Jaguars for export markets.

Original launch brochure from 1982.

VP had chrome grille surround and bright coachline.

But in April 1982, a very different kind of Vanden Plas was born – the Metro.

The rationale behind it was similar to that which had spawned the Allegro VP in 1974, though the Allegro name was never used; it was simply called the Vanden Plas 1500. The Metro, however, proudly bore the name of Leyland's chart-topping supermini. It was a trend that would continue across other models, including the Maestro, Montego and 200 Series, and would allow the Austin models to appeal to more traditional motorists, often wealthy older drivers who were used to the accoutrements of a larger, more luxurious car but no longer needed one.

It was initially offered in 1.3-litre guise only, with a choice of manual or automatic gearboxes. It was mechanically identical to the standard Metro, though a brake servo was fitted as standard.

Other equipment upgrades included bronze-tinted glass, along with bright inserts on the rubbing strips and window surrounds. Chrome door handles and VP motifs on the rear quarter panel and hub caps were further standouts, along with chrome wheel rim embellishers.

The radiator grille was dark grey with stainless steel edging, while wraparound bumpers and a tilt-slide sunroof completed the exterior styling.

Inside, it got 'Raschelle' crushed velvet interior, a unique brown fascia in lieu of the standard black, a rev counter and wooden door cappings, while a radio-cassette player also came as standard. It also got a three-spoke steering wheel, padded head restraint inserts, a digital clock and colour-keyed seatbelts.

Additional Vanden Plas script was added to tailgate.

Leather-trimmed wheel and rev counter were VP features.

It was a likeable and well-appointed little car and while some Vanden Plas traditionalists hated it for devaluing the brand, when viewed as a posh supermini it was a great little car, even if it was ambitiously priced at more than you'd pay for an Allegro 1.7 HL.

New seats and head restraints came along in 1983, but otherwise – and with the notable exception of the VP 500 (SEE PANEL) – the Vanden Plas continued unchanged until the 1984 Metro facelift. At that time, the VP received more wood, with walnut-style trim being added to the dashboard. Other improvements included thicker-pile carpets and over mats, along with the addition of leather trim to the options list.

Externally, body-coloured bumpers and flush-fitting wheel trims were added, while electric windows, central locking, new velour seats and remotely adjustable door mirrors completed the enhanced specification.

Aside from the VP 500, the rarest Metro Vanden Plases are three-door models made from March 1984. The arrival of the five-door body in October saw three-door Vanden Plas models discontinued, which also allowed Austin-Rover to subtly increase the price.

In 1987, a further option was added in the form of two-tone paint (silver and metallic grey, red and metallic grey or blue and silver), separated by the chrome-embellished coachline, along with restyled wheel trims.

Those with manual gearboxes also got a power increase, benefitting from the 71 bhp engine from the MG Metro but without its close-ratio gearbox, although the automatic model retained the previous 62 bhp set-up.

The final Vanden Plas Metros came off the line in 1988 and the brand died with them, though it did make a brief reappearance on a stretched version of the Rover 75 in 2004.

Two-tone paint was a late eighties option.

Late VPs had very refined cabins.

Later cars got stylised pinstripe.

Even the tailgate was two-tone.

The Vanden Plas 500

With the half-millionth Metro coming off the production line in late 1983, Austin-Rover decided to celebrate the milestone by producing a special edition of just 500 models.

The Metro Vanden Plas 500 was black with oatmeal leather seats, a gold coachline and 'VP500' emblems on the rear wings. They were fitted with the 'pepperpot' alloy wheels from the MG Metro, but with exclusive VP centre caps. A top-quality radio cassette player was also included – the height of in-car entertainment in 1983.

Each car was individually numbered with 1 to 500 etched on the front driver's side door window, while each one also came with a bottle of Moet & Chandon champagne and a mandate for the supplying dealer to put out a press release of the handover, much to the bemusement of the (often elderly and well-heeled) customer.

Today, there are five VP500s believed to still exist, though of these only three are roadworthy. One – an ex-museum car with less than 1,000 miles on the clock – sold for £12,125 including premium at Anglia Car Auctions in the UK in September 2018.

As a footnote, the millionth Metro, which was produced in 1986, never saw a special edition named after it. But it was a Vanden Plas and was given away as part of a phone-in competition on the BBC *Wogan* television programme to raise funds for the Children in Need charity. Its whereabouts is unknown.

CHAPTER 10

The MG Metros

While there were plans to create a performance version of the Metro from early on in the car's life, it would be May 1982 before that car appeared, and it would also bring with it the return of one of the most famous sporting names in the car industry.

Eighteen months prior as part of the Leyland Cars restructure, the company's new boss, Michael Edwardes, had made the difficult decision to close down the MG factory at Abingdon and with it went the famous marque, though BL was always keen to express it was a temporary hiatus.

This was, of course, true but dyed-in-the-wool MG aficionados were somewhat offended by the way in which the famous octagon returned not on a sports car, but on a mildly souped-up version of the Metro.

Ironically, the Metro was a better car dynamically than any factory standard MG Midget or MGB, but the fact that the new MG was based on a shopping car left many of them crying into their pints of Old Speckled Hen.

Yet the Metro was more than a badge-engineering exercise, unlike the MG variants of BMC saloons in the 1960s.

Above left: Metro marked the return of an iconic brand.

Above right: It was hardly a sports car, but MG was back.

Rather a bold claim...

Early MGs differed little externally.

A striking design.

First of all, it looked different with a rear spoiler-cum-window trim that enveloped the rear glass, along with 'pepperpot' alloy wheels and side graphics, while inside the sports seats were much improved. There were sports instruments, too, along with red carpets and seatbelts and a three-spoke steering wheel.

An increased compression ratio upped the power output to 72 bhp, while other positive features included four-piston brake calipers that were among the best on any small car. Shorter gearing meant it also felt much more eager than a standard Metro, albeit at the expense of being less refined at speed, a situation not helped by the lack of a five-speed gearbox.

A year later, the MG would evolve into a more serious hot hatch, with help of some engineering expertise from Lotus Cars Race Engineering – the team behind the turbocharged Lotus F1 cars. Enter the MG Metro Turbo, launched in August 1983.

By fitting a turbo to the Metro, not only would it make the car a livelier hot hatchback, but it would also allow Austin-Rover (as it was now known) to homologate a turbocharged model for motorsport.

The engine was fitted with a Garrett T3 turbo on a specially designed and cast exhaust manifold, with compressed air delivered to a single SU carburettor that was modified to run with pressurised air, thanks to variable rate fuel pressure delivery to ensure it didn't

Above left: The famous octagon.

Above right: Pepperpot alloys were a 1980s fad.

Metro turbo got extra body styling.

Sports seats, red carpets and a leather sports wheel.

flood. The unit was significantly strengthened with materials and processes common to competition engines and came with many Turbo-only parts, such as a ported cylinder head, pistons, crankshaft, block and sodium-filled exhaust valves, though aside from the hard-to-ignore turbo it looked little different from a standard A-Plus engine.

It was distinguishable from non-turbo models by its body kit, consisting of a front spoiler, wheel arch extensions and side skirts, along with flat-faced 13-inch alloy wheels with low-profile tyres.

Peak power was a rather modest sounding 93 bhp, though racing Metros could often muster double this. In road use, though, any more power would have been too much for the four-speed gearbox, especially as the transmission was lubricated by the engine oil.

As a result, one of the cleverest features of the Metro Turbo was an electronically controlled leak-off system from the turbo's wastegate, which would expel air from a valve in the turbo hose if the intake pressure was above 4 psi when running below 4,000 rpm, but would allow it to increase to 7 psi at faster engine speeds, where peak torque was already surpassed. This early iteration of what's now largely regarded as boost control was quite innovative technology and exists in most turbocharged cars today. It didn't, however, address the problem it was intended to address, and although it prevented boost arriving at the same time as peak torque, the gearbox failures it was meant to alleviate still came thick and fast.

That is, of course, if the Metro was moving at all. At launch, there was a problem with the enamel-coated alloys, which were too shiny and would cause the tyres to slip around

Facelift MGs got coloured keyed bumpers and wheel trims.

1987 MG Metro Turbo

An MG Rover Group image for editorial purposes only

Later Turbos were more subtle.

65

the beads, which in extreme cases, under hard acceleration, would make the wheels turn but not the tyres, or the terrifying opposite under braking.

In 1984, the MG models took on the changes from the rest of the Metro range including the vastly improved one-piece dashboard and revised seats, while in 1986 the spoiler and bodykits became colour keyed.

Metric wheels and tyres were fitted as per the standard Metro models, with a new design and the option of silver or white alloys depending on body colour, though a cost-cutting exercise in 1987 saw the alloy wheels being moved over to the options list as an upsell opportunity for dealers. Instead, the MG got stylised hubcaps in silver with the MG logo picked out in red, while if you ordered a white MG Metro you got white trims instead.

Red piping ran through the interior, it was even on the gear knob.

Red seatbelts were an MG saloon car theme.

Under the bonnet was pure A-Series.

In 1988, to coincide with the newly formed Rover Group, the MG got a final restyle, with new and improved seats and distinctive side graphics, with large 'floating' MG badges down the sides and new, rather lovely, multi-spoke alloy wheels.

But while the last-of-the-line MG Metros looked great, they felt crudely engineered compared to their rivals of the day. The Peugeot 205 GTi and Renault 5 GT Turbo, to name but two, did things so much better.

With the demise of the A-Series models in 1990 came the demise of the MG Metro, after 120,197 standard models and 21,968 Turbos had been built. The following year the MG badge would once again take a sabbatical until it returned in 1995 with the MGF. This time, the traditionalists got what they wanted; a rear-drive sports car and not a red seatbelt in sight.

Chin spoiler and lattice alloys mark this out as a late Turbo.

MG octagons adorned the car's flanks.

Subtle MG badges on tailgate.

Chapter 11

The GTa and GTi

The idea of a non-MG sporting Metro was first tested for the 1988 model year to coincide with the formation of Rover Group and its future plans for the MG brand.

In many ways the Metro GTa was ahead of its time, too. It was one of the first real 'warm' hatches, with all the looks of its sportier sibling, but not the performance. In an era where people's car choices were becoming increasingly dictated to by ever-increasing insurance premiums, it hit a sweet spot.

The GTa, then, was mechanically the same as the standard Metro 1.3 GS, other than it had shorter gear ratios.

But while it wasn't much quicker, it certainly looked the part, with the sports seats, side skirts, spoilers and lattice alloy wheels from the last pre-Rover era Metros.

Available in a limited number of (usually vibrant) colours, the Metro GTa was an extremely popular choice with younger drivers and helped shore-up sales at a time where Metro was struggling, as well as to draw in younger buyers to the company.

It was no surprise, then, to see the GTa continue as a new model in the 1990 Rover Metro line-up, using a 75 bhp version of the 1.4-litre K-Series and with a similar trim level to the vaguely sporting S, but with the addition of GTa badges, red seatbelts and sports

Above left: MG meets GTi. (Metro Owners Club)

Above right: At first glance, a GTa could easily pass for an MG Turbo.

seats. It wasn't quite as bold as the previous GTa, though, with alloys only offered as an option (though the standard steel wheels had quite sporty-looking trims) and black plastic bumpers with red piping, as opposed to body-coloured.

Not only did this keep GTa insurance premiums sensible at a time where hot hatches were rapidly disappearing, both from model ranges and from people's driveways, but it also left the path clear for Rover to introduce a hotter model as a successor to the Metro Turbo.

Unperturbed by the challenges laid out by spiralling insurance and hot hatchbacks falling out of fashion, Rover continued unabashed and the Metro GTi 16v appeared shortly after the R6 launch. Its power output of 95 bhp (later 103 bhp) might not sound much, but when you consider it was powering a car that was lighter and smaller than most of its rivals, along with the K-Series engine's reputation for peppy mid-range torque, you had a car that was much more than the sum of its parts.

Not only did it look great, with the alloy wheels from the Rover 216GTi and a handsome interior with deeply bolstered sports seats, but it was also huge fun to drive, fully exploiting the improvements that Rover had made by adopting interlinked Hydragas for the new-generation Metro.

The GTi 16v was quicker from 0–60 mph than a contemporary Volkswagen Golf GTi and an easy match for a Peugeot 205 GTi 1.6. Indeed, in more recent times it has become one of the forgotten greats. A hot hatchback that you don't realise is any good until you get the pleasure; and a pleasure it certainly is.

Above left: GTa had 1.4 K-Series.

Above right: 16v GTi could out-accelerate a Golf GTi.

Right: GTa SE was plainer than previous sporty Metros.

ROVER METRO GTa SE

RGS/1094/497

ROVER   A Rover Cars External Affairs (031 792 8000) photograph. Copyright free for editorial purposes only. For any other use, prior written permission is required.

CHAPTER 12

Going Topless – The Metro Convertibles

While convertors such as Crayford and Rapport were lopping the top off Metros from very early on in its life, the car had almost become the Rover 100 by the time an official factory ragtop was introduced.

That car was part of a strategy by Rover Group to grow its business through targeting niches, which is why we also saw Coupe and Cabriolet versions of the R8 200, along with the less successful 800 Coupe.

It was first revealed at the 1992 Berlin Motor Show having been developed alongside the Mini convertible, but LAMM – the company behind the conversions – went bust, leaving Rover to outsource the rest of the development to Tickford.

In the end, it was 1994 before the Metro Cabriolet went into production, and only around 200 were made before the Metro morphed into the 100, making it one of the rarest Metro variants ever.

It's not a car that was actively marketed by Rover either, as it soon became apparent that it was an expensive car to build, and that meant it attracted a list price in the UK of almost £13,000.

Above left: Original Metro Cabriolet is a rare car today.

Above right: Rover's press photo subtly hides huge tonneau cover with a bunch of flowers.

Eagle-eyed enthusiasts will notice that despite being a three-door, the Metro/100 Cabriolet has its fuel filler toward the back of the rear wing as opposed to being ahead of the wheel arch as on three-door models.

That's because it was based on the platform of the five-door model to allow room for extra strengthening in the sills to avoid body flex, meaning it was a far more complex engineering exercise than it would first appear. Additional metal was also added to the bulkhead, along with stiffened A-pillars.

At the rear, a stronger shell and strengthened boot lid and parcel shelf added a modicum of rollover protection, as did the rather pram-like folded roof and tonneau. Indeed, the roof was a cause of much strife within Rover as the original supplier couldn't meet quality control standards, leading Rover to switch suppliers for 1995. That's why early cars have black roofs and later ones, grey.

While early cars had a choice of manual or electric roofs, those made from 1995 had electric-only. The 100 Convertible, as it was by then, is therefore unique in being the only car ever to be fitted with electric rear windows when they weren't even offered as an option in the front.

These arc into the rear side of the car as the roof itself raises, folds and sits itself down where the glass previously was; it's a fascinatingly (needlessly?) complex operation that was undoubtedly expensive to engineer.

As a result, the list price was almost as expensive as the entry-level 200 Cabriolet at £12,621, but it seems that Rover hit on a very clever way of getting around the VAT element of this by selling cars through its dealership in St Helier, Jersey, as 'used' examples with little more than delivery miles, which could then be re-imported tax-free. Even then, they cost the lion's share of £10,000 and, understandably, that was too much for most buyers.

Fun and funky as it was, the Metro/100 Cabrio was also a folly at a time when Rover needed it least, and a fairly expensive engineering exercise that is said to have completely baffled its new German owner, BMW, which reportedly said it would have canned the Metro Cabrio at the design stage.

Rover 100 cabrio
in Flame Red.

CHAPTER 13

Commercially Viable? – Metro Vans and Pick-ups

As well as being a supermini, the Metro also found reasonable success as a commercial vehicle, especially with fleets that had a need for smaller vans, such as local Royal Mail deliveries, meter readers, couriers and car parts suppliers.

The Metrovan, as it was first known, was introduced in 1982 and was initially sold not as an Austin, but as a Morris, as until the latter brand's demise in 1985 it was the name that Leyland used for its commercial vehicles.

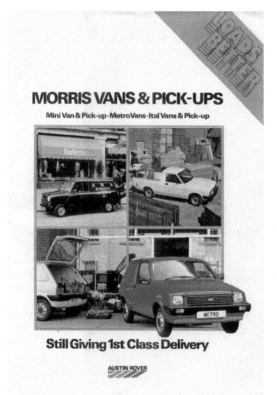

Above: A rental TV and a Metro van – welcome to 1980s Britain.

Left: As a van, the Metro was sold as a Morris.

The Morris Metrovan was sold alongside the Mini Van and Pick-up and Ital Van and Pick-up and was a surprisingly useful little van, a result of the Metro's excellent interior packaging and class-leading load space as a passenger car. The Metrovan came as a 1.0- or 1.3-litre, as per the passenger car range.

In 1985, with the Morris brand breathing its last, the Metrovan was rebranded. The 1.0-litre model became the Austin Metro 310 Van and the 1.3 became the 510 Van. Both took on the spec of the Metro City unless further options were specified, so came with vinyl seats and a very basic cabin, though L-spec upgrades were available on special-build orders. The famous London department store, Harrods, owned a fleet which it had trimmed in a bespoke cloth to uphold the aspirational nature of its brand.

One of only a handful of pre-facelift Metro vans known to still exist.

Note the New Metro in the showroom in Rover promotional image.

The load bay was surprisingly useful. (KGF Classic Cars)

The Metro Van lived on into the Rover Metro years, as three-door Metro shells were still being produced to keep automatic models in production until the CVT arrived in 1992 but was eventually killed off when the pre-Rover Metros ceased production. A van version of the Rover Metro/100 never appeared, but the basic concept was revisited in 2003, with MG Rover introducing the 25-based Rover Commerce; a van that was loosely based on a derivative of a car designed to replace the Metro eight years earlier.

When it introduced the Metrovan, Austin-Rover also briefly considered the idea of a Metro pick-up, with its main London dealer group, Broadfields, developing a prototype to test fleet interest. Two were supposedly made – one white, one red – but despite being evaluated by Austin-Rover senior management, the cost of the project was considered too much for the relatively small volumes.

Left: Functional but comfortable was the order of the day. (KGF Classic Cars)

Below: Six-year corrosion warranty was a brave move!

The pick-up idea was briefly revisited in 1984, after the UK Ports Authority expressed an interest in a small British pick-up. Dibden Purlieu Motors of Southampton commissioned a local conversion and tried to convince Austin-Rover to back it, without much success. The truck used a GRP rear body and was 'very well executed' according to *Commercial Motor* magazine, which road tested it.

But despite Dibden Purlieu's initial optimism, claiming there was 'an enormous demand for small European pick-ups', it never went further.

A late model Metro 310. (KGF Classic Cars)

Metric steel wheels remained even after the Metro car was revised. (KGF Classic Cars)

A Metro pick-up on test. (RBI)

CHAPTER 14

Metro Might-Have-Beens

We've covered the ECV3, AR6 and R6X elsewhere, but there were other Metro variants that never made production. Here are the key ones.

Metro Saloon

A three-box saloon was part of the Metro plan from early on right up until the LC8 emergency restyle, getting as far as a nearly finished prototype before Leyland's senior management pulled the plug. At least one prototype still exists and is stored at the British Motor Museum in Gaydon, Warwickshire, UK.

The Metro saloon prototype.

Saloon prototype from the rear.

The Alcan Metro.

Alcan Metro

Built by aluminium giant ALCAN, better known for making drinks cans, the ALCAN MG Metro was produced as a feasibility study for a new lightweight bodyshell, as pushed for by Leyland's then product chief, Spen King, a former Land Rover man who was conversant with alloy technologies. It was rejected on cost grounds.

Pedestrian Safety Car 1

PSC1, as it was known for short, experimented with technology that's commonplace today but was unheard of in 1986, when it was first seen. It was developed at a cost of over £1 million by the Transport and Road Research Laboratory. Its bonnet was designed to deform on impact and absorb pedestrian impacts, though its drooping nose was challenging to look at.

Pedestrian Safety Car PSC1. (AROnline)

The Metro Scout.

Metro Scout

The Rover Metro Scout was designed and built by Automotive Development Consultants (ADC) in 1991, a company which had already been involved with Rover Group via various MG roadster proposals. However, the Scout was something different and, with the benefit of hindsight, was years ahead of its time.

A standard Rover Metro was fitted with a taller roof, a higher side-hinged tailgate, bigger rear side windows, roof rails, extra plastic panels, headlamps guards and even an externally mounted spare wheel in order to resemble a mini-4 x 4. But had Rover been brave enough to launch its crossover, would it ever have been the commercial success that such types of vehicle went on to become?

Metro 'SP'

Rover Special Products, or RSP, was an in-house unit responsible for a number of low-volume projects including the original decision to bring back the Mini Cooper in 1990. The Metro 'SP' was a plan to create a proper hot hatch version of the Rover Metro GTi with circa 120 bhp and a turbocharged K-Series. Its bodykit was styled by Steve Harper, who penned the Ford Escort RS Cosworth, and it featured a number of similar styling cues. While there was plenty of excitement for the concept within the company, sadly none of it came from budget-holders.

The Metro SP.
(AROnline)

78

Metro Ranger

As well as the dealer conversions mentioned elsewhere, there was one Metro pick-up that was created internally, though it wasn't aimed at the commercial vehicle market. The Metro Ranger was a leisure-market 'lifestyle' vehicle, not dissimilar in concept to the Talbot-Matra Rancho.

It got roof-mounted spotlights, nudge bars and all-weather rough terrain tyres. It was a pretty funky thing and low volume production was considered, but sadly the numbers in the business plan simply didn't add up.

The Metro Ranger.

CHAPTER 15

Weird and Wonderful – Metro Convertors

Tickford styling study.

The Metro was such a well-known car that it was inevitable there would be a few aftermarket conversions, some more successful than others. Here are some of the best-known examples.

Crayford

The Crayford 'Metro Politan' was killed off very quickly as, despite a long-standing relationship with BL, the company was contracted by Ford to build the Fiesta 'Fly' convertible instead. Only a handful of Crayford Metro Politans were made.

Crayford Metro-politan.

The Metro Cooper.

Cooper/Monaco

John Cooper Garages set to work on the Metro very early on, preparing a 'Cooper' model that had Wolfrace alloy wheels very similar to those that would appear on the MG. It had twin carburettors and a fast-flow exhaust. The model was renamed the 'Metro Monaco' at Leyland's request so as not to impact MG Metro sales.

Frazer Tickford

Developed alongside Aston Martins, the Frazer Tickford was an extra-luxurious performance version of the Metro with a bespoke wide-arch bodykit. It cost three times as much as a Metro S and a total of twenty-six were completed.

The Frazer Tickford Metro.

The Janspeed Metro. (AROnline)

Janspeed

Janspeed created a Metro Turbo before the Austin-Rover did, its aftermarket conversion adding a twin-choke Dellorto carburettor. It could do 0–60 mph in under nine seconds.

Turbo Technics

The Turbo Technics Metro was less extreme than the Janspeed and also a whole lot more subtle. It had a Garret T3 turbocharger and side graphics but retained the standard Metro wheels.

Metro Turbo Technics.

Wood and Pickett Metro Plus.

Wood and Pickett

Wood and Pickett had made its name as a Mini convertor, but in 1980 surprised everyone – not least BL – by revealing its 'Laser' Metro at the same motorshow as the Metro itself in October 1980. The W&P model had a body kit, leather trim, air conditioning, cruise control, Wilton carpets and an electric sunroof, as well as a RayJay turbocharger.

A less well-appointed 'Metro Plus' appeared a year later, retaining the turbocharger but with fewer luxury appointments.

Chairman

One of the more unusual but also most popular Metro conversions came in the form of the Chairman, created by Gowrings Mobility. Gowrings was one of the pioneers of wheelchair accessible vehicles and it still is today. It converted Metros from early Austin models right through to 100s, by removing the rear bodywork and fitting a GRP-moulded raised back body, with a horsebox-style rear door that folded down to create ramped access to the rear.

The tall and boxy rear end earned it the nickname 'Popemobile' and in later life Metro Chairmans became quite popular with those who wanted a small but capacious van – itself a missed opportunity, perhaps?

The Metro Chairman.

Rapport

The Rapport Metrosport was the first soft-top Metro and retained its rigidity by keeping the B-pillars and side panels of the original car, a bit like a Citroen 2CV. Despite the cost-cutting approach, the look was quite harmonious.

The Rapport Metrosport.

CHAPTER 16

Metro in Motorsport

Back in the eighties, almost every car manufacturer was involved in motorsport and Leyland Cars was no exception, with the 'Unipart Metro Challenge' beginning as early as the 1981 season.

'At the time of Metro's development, we were involved with BL Special Tuning, which was an aftermarket parts business,' BL's Director of Motorsport, John Davenport, told *Autosport* in 1982. 'It wasn't until we started to develop tuning parts for the Metro that we really started to see its competition potential.'

Turbos regularly produced over 250 bhp.

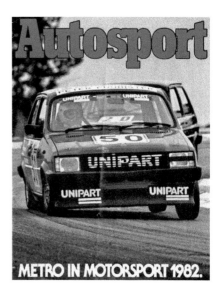

Motor sport was part of the Metro plan from day one.

BL Motorsport developed a 'Performance Pack' for the Metro aimed at privateer racers, and the Metro Challenge was born, won in its first year by Steve Soper, who went on to become one of the best-known names in touring car racing.

Leyland also competed in the British Saloon Car Championship with its works backed 'Datapost' Metros.

In 1983, to coincide with the launch of the MG Metro, the series was rebranded to become the MG Metro Challenge, which in turn morphed into the MG Car Club's MG Metro Cup in 1992, a series that's still going today and plays host to many of those original cars from the eighties.

The launch of the MG Metro also saw Austin-Rover venturing bravely into the British Touring Car Championship with an MG Metro Turbo, which allegedly developed in excess of 200 bhp. Of the five works cars made, three of them were restored in the mid-2000s by former Austin Rover works driver Patrick Watts, who now drives them in historic motorsport events and invites other famous racers to compete in them, too.

One of Patrick Watts's restored MG turbos in historic touring car action.

Works MG Metro race team, *c.* 1984.

But the BTCC campaign was short-lived, with Austin-Rover unable to resist the allure of Group B rallying, leading to the birth of the legendary MG Metro 6R4, to which we've dedicated a chapter of its own.

In 1991, Rover once again used motorsport to promote its new Metro, coming up with a fascinating motorsport concept in the form of the RoverSport Dunlop Metro GTi Challenge, which combined the disciplines of circuit racing, hill-climbing and rallying, bringing with it a field of drivers with experience of both.

The challenge series ran until 1994 but was canned after the BMW takeover.

Dunlop Metro Challenge cars were supplied as basic cars to competitors.

Tony Pond at the wheel on the Isle of Man.

Rover dealer and rally driver David Gillanders was one of the series' competitors.

CHAPTER 17

The 6R4

The 6R4 (which stood for V6, Rear-engine, 4-wheel-drive) was a Metro in name and visual similarity only and developed to compete in 'Group B' super rallying. It retained the Metro's windscreen, headlights and basic proportions, but was built upon a tubular spaceframe chassis.

The decision to use the Metro was simple. Not only was it the Austin-Rover car of the moment, but it was also short, which meant a rally version could come with a wide track yet be small enough to be thrown sideways around forest stages.

Above: Tony Pond on the 1985 Lombard RAC Rally.

Left: 6R4 is popular in historic rallying today.

John Davenport, head of Austin-Rover Motorsport, brought in the engineering team at Williams F1 to help, with the company's design chief, Patrick Head, leading the project.

While most Group B cars were adopting turbocharged four-cylinder engines, Davenport decided his Metro should have a larger capacity, naturally aspirated engine, thus avoiding problems with turbo lag and higher running temperatures. A Honda V6 was considered, based on the 2.7-litre 24-valve unit destined for the Rover 800, but Head wanted something smaller and lighter.

So while ex-Cosworth man David Wood set about designing a compact, aluminium-alloy 3-litre V6 (called 'V64V' because of its V6 configuration with 4 valves per cylinder), a temporary engine was created by lopping two cylinders off a 3.5-litre Rover V8 to help develop the rest of the car.

The MG Metro 6R4 made its debut at London's Excelsior Hotel in February 1984, and in dramatic style. The event began with the gathered journalists being invited to watch a film of a prototype undergoing testing. As the film reached its climax, the car was driven towards the camera, and just as it became life-size on the cinema screen, a real 6R4 burst through it, the driver – Tony Pond – bringing the car to a halt just short of the astonished crowd.

Two engines were developed. Domestic, with around 250 bhp, and international with 400 bhp, enabling the car to hit 60 mph from rest in just 3.2 seconds, and 100 mph in 8.2 seconds.

Scottish rally ace Jimmy McRae puts the 6R4 through its paces in 1986.

Cabin of a 6R4 road car.

In March 1985 the 6R4 took its first win, at the Gwynedd Rally, and by October that year the 200 cars required to homologate the super-Metro for the World Rally Championship had been built. The 6R4 continued to evolve, with reliability problems impacting its early rally career. But just as it started to show promise, with Tony Pond taking third place in the 1985 Lombard RAC Rally, the FIA announced the end of Group B rallying following a series of fatal accidents.

Austin Rover pulled out of motorsport in 1987 and sold off its stock of 6R4s by reducing the original £45,000 asking price to just £16,000. It also sold the design of the V64V engine to TWR, in whose hands it evolved into a 3.5-litre twin-turbo unit that appeared in the Jaguar XJ220 supercar.

Many 6R4s, along with other Group B racers, went on to be used in privateer rallycross events.

Above left: Tony Pond's ex-works car on show in 2018.

Above right: Most of the 6R4s made still survive and are regularly campaigned.

Left: 6R4 on a hill-climb at Goodwood.

CHAPTER 18

Metro in Miniature – How Corgi Toys Developed its Own Metro in Secret

There was an air of secrecy across Longbridge as the final 'LC8' Metro took shape, but those secrets were well known 150 miles down the road in Swansea, South Wales, where another team of engineers were working on a secret Metro project of their own.

Over at the headquarters of toy manufacturer Mettoy, was a room full of secret drawings and photographs from which the team behind the Corgi Toys brand worked to produce not just one, but two Metros in time for the 1980 British Motor Show.

The cars would be 1:64 scale and 1:36 scale replicas of the Metro and would be given away at the Motor Show and through Austin-Morris dealers, as well as to employees and their families at a Metro-themed Longbridge family day during the October half-term break. Indeed, the 1:64 scale toys in 'Longbridge Family Day Souvenir' boxes are highly sought-after today.

All of the Corgi
Metros from 1981.

The other models came in fully covered boxes with lift-up flaps, as opposed to the more common window boxes of the day, which were fully liveried in Metro advertising material. 'A British Car to Beat the World' graced one panel and a Metro under a Union Jack dust sheet with 'This Could Be Your Finest Hour' was on the other, as the front of the car being peeked out under the sheet as if it were about to be revealed.

The larger and smaller scale models came in similar packaging with a choice of red or blue paint, both of which were produced in similar numbers and are still quite common today.

The smaller model is pretty basic, but the larger one was extremely well detailed for its time, with the rear lights picked out in red, a separate bumper moulding and silver headlamps. The Metro came with opening doors and a hatchback, which even had a 'Metro HLS' badge stamped into the metal. The front seats tilted forward and the rear ones were split folding in order to highlight some of the features that made the Metro itself such an advanced car for its time.

Eventually, both toys became part of the standard Corgi toys range, with the toymaker hitting on another clever sales ploy in 1981, producing a special edition purple Metro to celebrate the wedding of the most famous Metro owner of all, Lady Diana Spencer, to Prince Charles. It became one of the company's best-selling toys of all-time.

Both of the scale Metros remained part of the Corgi Toys range until well into the 1990s, with multiple different themes including the Datapost rally and circuit cars. It survived during a period of industrial unrest and financial struggles that was as difficult for Corgi as it was for Austin-Rover.

Launch model was available in red or blue.

Promotional box had cut-outs to hold wheels in place.

CHAPTER 19

Buying a Metro Today

Whichever Metro you choose,
they're all a joy to drive.

It was a car that touched millions of lives and achieved over 2 million sales during its lifetime, so it's of little surprise that the Metro is rapidly developing a cult following among classic car enthusiasts.

Its low running costs and accessible purchase price also make it popular among younger enthusiasts, many of whom are more youthful than the Metros they own and cherish.

But while a Metro is a simple and largely enjoyable choice of classic car, there are a few things you need to look out for:

Rust

While the Metro was quite advanced for its time, one area where Leyland didn't move the game forward as much as it claimed was in the area of rust protection. While all Metro panels were dipped in a zinc-primer for protection, the car came with a number of natural rust traps, the most common being the front and rear edges of the sills, the subframes and their mounting points and – on Mk I Metros – the front wings, which had a moisture trap between the headlights and the inner wing structure that would eventually manifest itself as a vertical stripe of rust down each front wing. It was a common sight on Metros in the late eighties and early nineties, though the saving grace was that the wings themselves were a bolt-on repair.

Other areas where corrosion was common were the seam between the front valance and lower part of the front wing, the boot floor and the seam where the roof and tailgate would meet, as moisture would gather around the boot hinges and eventually trigger rust.

Rover got on top of the front end corrosion when the Rover Metro appeared, but in redesigning the rear quarter of the car to have a more rounded appearance, it inadvertently created a brand new rust trap inside the rear wheel arch which would cause muck to build up inside the wheel arch lip. Rotten rear arches on Rover Metros and 100s are so common that repair sections were (and still are) cheap and plentiful on the used market. Luckily, rust here is rarely structural, so it's a cosmetic issue alone.

Of far greater concern is corrosion to the rear of the sills, which seems to affect Rover versions more so than the Austin and MG models, which were more prone to front-end corrosion.

Front wing rust is common on early cars.

Rear sills can rot out and repairs can be complex due to petrol tank location.

Rear wheel arch corrosion is common on Rover Metros and 100s.

Engines

Mechanically, all Metro variants are fairly simple. The A-Plus engines, like the A-Series before them, are an absolute doddle to work on and because of the engine's longevity and use in other BL cars, parts are still very easy to get hold of.

They tend to get smoky with age and can suffer from timing chain wear (listen for a chattering noise at idle), but there's nothing there that's beyond the remit of the skilled home mechanic, other than perhaps the more complex installation of the Turbo models.

K-Series engined cars are more advanced and use electronic ignition and often fuel injection too, but the K is also an easy engine to work on with most major components easily accessible. The engine's Achilles' Heel is its well-known reputation for head gasket failure, which affects 16v models more so than 8v ones, though this is usually predicated by a leak from the inlet manifold gasket which causes the coolant level to drop in the first place.

For this reason some buyers are terrified of the K-Series engine, even though replacing the head gasket and skimming the head is no more than half-a-day's work for a competent garage and won't ever result in a huge bill.

A-Series engine is simple and easy to maintain.

K-Series is prone to head gasket failure so check coolant level carefully.

Bruised and battered, but still well-loved.

Running gear

Hydragas suspension units, both early systems and later front-to-rear interconnected set-ups, are generally reliable, though they do suffer from pressure loss over time. A Metro that sits low to the ground is therefore in need of a pump-up, but because the MGF uses Metro-derived subframes and suspension most MG specialists have the necessary equipment to give your Metro a top-up and it's a quick and inexpensive job.

Brakes are simple and are shared with other BL and Rover cars, with cheap and plentiful parts supply.

That leaves transmissions. The gearbox-in-sump arrangement of the A-Series powered cars requires regular oil changes to keep healthy, or it can suffer from bearing wear and – ultimately – failure. Again, though, it's not too onerous a fix, while transmission whine is almost a standard feature of early Metros.

Later cars have a much sharper gearchange, with the R65 transmission based on a Peugeot-Citroen designed unit. The gearbox is pretty tough and will usually last the life of the car.

Interiors and trim

While trim and interior parts are unlikely to ever stop you enjoying your car, they can be among the most irritating faults and the most difficult to solve, especially if you like to keep your Metro in tip-top condition.

Interior fabrics are prone to wear both with age and use, while plastic bits of trim both internal and external are getting very difficult to find. Some new old-stock bits occasionally appear at specialists or on online auction sites, however. For the detail-driven enthusiast, though, tracking down that elusive part will either be a source of constant frustration or a part of the fun.

The end of the road but breakers can be a good source of spares.